GW00697124

STALIN

© EDIMAT BOOKS Ltd. London
is an affiliate of Edimat Libros S.A.
C/ Primavera, 35 Pol. Ind. El Malvar
Arganda del Rey - 28500 (Madrid) Spain
E-mail: edimat@edimat.es

Title: *Stalin*
In charge of the Work:
Francisco Luis Cardona Castro
*Doctor in History by the Barcelona University
and Professor*
Coordination of texts:
*Manuel Giménez Saurina, Manuel Mas Franch
and Miguel Giménez Saurina*

ISBN: 84-9794-019-9
Legal Deposit: M-48872-2004

PRINTED IN SPAIN

INTRODUCTION

At the end of September, 1939, an editor from the magazine Life travelled to Coyoacán to entrust Trotsky with the writing of two articles – one about Stalin's temperament, and another on the death of Lenin. When the editor collected the articles on his return to Mexico he was very pleased with them. So, apparently, was Trotsky, apart from one thing: according to the editor's own words, Leon Trotsky had omitted to explain the important fact that Stalin had poisoned Lenin.

Trotsky was therefore asked to write a third article. However when this one arrived on the editor's desk in New York, it was also rejected. In the end, it was published by the Liberty, a newspaper in the Hearst chain, on 10th August 1940, exactly ten days before Trotsky was assassinated on the Stalin's orders.

The article was entitled "Did Stalin Administer Poison to Lenin?" but the truth is that Trotsky's article leaves the controversy unanswered and the question in the air, without even attempting to provide any evidence to substantiate his theory.

In the article all that Trotsky says is that Lenin had asked Stalin to provide him with a poison so that, in the event of being overcome in an attack, he would be able to take his own life. And Stalin had communicated the request to The Politburo in the presence of Trotsky, Zinoviev and Kamenev. Trotsky points out in the article that Lenin may have wanted to test Stalin with this request: to what extent would Stalin have liked to take advantage of the opportunity?

However, Trotsky never gave any evidence, apart from stating that Stalin communicated Lenin's request to The Politburo, that the meeting between Stalin and Lenin took place. According to the article, Lenin was already against Stalin when he asked for the poison on the 23rd February, 1923. He had even written a political statement requesting that Stalin be replaced as Secretary General of the Party.

So is it possible that Stalin forced Lenin's doctors to administer him poison? Or even that he forced Lenin's own family to do it? As we will see further on, Joseph Stalin was a man capable of either possibility. However, the illness that took hold of Lenin before the end of that February of 1923, and which lasted all through March and right up until the day of his death in January 1924, never showed any signs of proving the hypothesis that Stalin was responsible for the death of Lenin.

Bibliography

ALLINLEVA, S.: *Vint cartes a un amic*, Barcelona, 1967.

BENOIT, J.: *Stalin*, Dopesa, Barcelona, 1974.

BOFFA, G.: *Stalin*, Orbis, Barcelona, 1985.

CARR, E. H.: *La revolución rusa: de Lenin a Stalin*, Alianza, Madrid, 1983.

D'ASIER, E.: *Stalin, ese desconocido*, Aymá, Barcelona, 1964.

DEUTSCHER, I.: *Stalin*, biografía política, Era, México, 1966.

ELLENSTEIN, J.: *El fenómeno estaliniano*, Laia, Barcelona, 1977.

FRANK, P.: *El stalinismo*, Fontamara, Barcelona, 1978.

GREY, IAN: *Stalin*, Salvat, Barcelona, 1989, 2 vols.

HILGAR, G.: *Stalin*, Moretón, Bilbao, 1968.

LUDWIG, E.: *Adalides de Europa, Stalin*, Juventud, Barcelona, 1935.

Medvedier, Z. A.: *Que juzgue la historia*, Destino, Barcelona, 1977.

Paine, R.: *Stalin*, Plaza y Janés, Barcelona, 1968.

Reinen, H.: *El nacimiento del estalinismo*, Critica, Barcelona, 1982.

Rodríguez Lázaro, J.: *Los últimos días de Stalin*, Petronio, Barcelona, 1976.

Stalin: *¿Anarquismo o socialismo?*, Siete y Media, Barcelona, 1978.

— *El Marxismo y la cuestión nacional*, Fundamentos, Barcelona, 1976.

— *Fundamentos del leninismo*, Akal, Madrid, 1975

— *Obra completa*, Vanguardia Obrera [Workers' Vanguard], Madrid, 1984, 10 vols.

— *Obras escogidas*, Emiliano Escolar, Madrid, 1977.

— *Historia de la Rusia soviética*, Alianza, Madrid, 1983, 4 Vols.

Ul, A. B.: *Stalin*, Noguer, Barcelona, 1975, 2 vols.

VV.AA. *Stalin*, Círculo de Amigos de la Historia, Madrid, 1975.

VV.AA. *Stalin*, Urbión, Madrid, 1984.

Werth, A.: *Rusia en la guerra (1940 - 1945)*, Barcelona, 1967, 2 vols.

CHAPTER I

A DICTATOR IS BORN

In a poor house at number 10 Cathedral Street, in the small town of Gori, in the Caucusus, on 21st December, 1879, Iosif Vissarionovich Dzhugashvili was born. He was to grow up to be Stalin, which in Russian means 'Man of Steel'.

What can we say about the town of Gori? It is a picturesque provincial town located on the banks of the River Kura, about 46 miles from Tiflis. It is one of the oldest towns in Georgia, founded, according to traditional belief, in the twelfth century by Armenians fleeing from the Turks.

The town streets wound vaguely around a collection of allotments, more like a small village than a town. In a small adobe and brick house with an earthen roof, little more than a shack, lived the Dzhugashvili family: Stalin's parents, Vissarion, who they called Beso, and Ekaterina, known as Keke. They were modest people, originating from families of serfs. Vissarion worked as a cobbler in a shoe factory, although before that he had laboured on the land, and Keke did domestic chores for other people to contribute to their meagre income, which Stalin's father spent mostly on vodka, doing justice to the Russian proverb 'to drink like a cobbler', and leaving just enough to put the daily stew on the table.

They were hard times for the little boy Iosif, who they called Soso. His father was more likely to be drunk than sober on the few occasions he was at home, and was prone to whip the little boy for the slightest triviality. His mother, however, protected and cared for him as best she could in their poverty. Soso was an only child, his mother having lost three children previously, and she made sure he was always clean and tidy and as well-fed as possible.

When Soso was five years old, his father left to work at the Adelkhanov shoe factory based in Tiflis, leaving a very relieved mother and child behind him. At seven, the child was strong enough to survive a terrible smallpox epidemic that struck Georgia. But the disease left its mark - both physically on his face, and on the child's future, for his mother made a promise to God during her son's illness that if he survived she would have him enter the clergy, this being a viable way for a peasant to ensure himself a future.

Soso's education

Once Iosif had recovered from the smallpox, his mother took him to the local parish priest to ask his advice on the matter. They were recommended a small religious institution in the town which provided an education for future seminarians. The only problem was that the school required its students to speak Russian, and Iosif only spoke Georgian. However, not to be daunted, Keke made several visits and succeeded in persuading one of their neighbours, called Charkviani, to teach the child the Russian alphabet.

Iosif possessed an extraordinary memory, and learnt the new language quickly, so that in September, 1888, not yet nine years old, he was enrolled at the religious institution in Gori. His mother, devoted to her son's future, managed to obtain a grant of three roubles a month for Iosif's education, and added to the money that she earned cleaning they had a reasonable living. Iosif's father had practically abandoned his family duties when he left home.

Iosiv Vissarionovitch, known as Stalin, 'the iron man'.

However, when six years later Vissarion learnt that his son had been awarded a study grant to attend the seminary of theology in Tiflis, he decided he was not in agreement with his wife's decision, and took Iosif away to work at his side in the shoe factory and learn the trade of shoemaker. Keke, however, furious with him, snatched her son back and reinstated him at the school in Gori.

Once back at the school, Iosif discovered that his Georgian teachers had been replaced by Russians; a change that caused tension among the students. Iosif often took a leading role in inciting his fellow students to rebellion.

Finally, after several incidents, which his teachers overlooked out of respect for his intelligence, Iosif took his final exams at fourteen years old. It was also about this time that Iosif's father died, the police informing his widow that he had ended his days as a vagabond.

Ian Grey, the author of a magnificent biography of the dictator, writes that information about Stalin's father is scarce. In 1885, he left his family for Tiflis, where he worked in a shoe factory owned by a man called Adelkhanov, an Armenian who had given him employment before his marriage. According to Grey, Stalin only once made public reference to his father, when he explained, understandably with no sign of affection, that his father had been 'not a true proletarian, for he possessed the mentality of a little bourgeois'. On another occasion Stalin mentioned his childhood and his parents in an interview granted to Emil Ludwig in 1931, when his biographies were enjoying great popularity. Ludwig asked him "What was it that prompted you to rebel? Was it due to the way your parents treated you?" and Stalin replied: "No, my parents were uneducated but they never treated me badly".

So why is this statement so different from other versions of his childhood? Perhaps to protect the memory of his mother, one of the few people he really loved, from the public eye.

14

Disproportionate affection for the mother: another example of the Oedipus Complex, Freud would say, just like Hitler, Napoleon, Franco and so many other dictators – and the antipathy for his father?

Iosif Iremashvili, one of Stalin's friends, wrote about the dictator's father: *He was well-built, with a black moustache and eyebrows (features shared by his son), he was stern and short-tempered by nature, traits which were aggravated by alcohol.* Georgians had a strong reputation for being heavy drinkers, and the expression 'to drink like a cobbler' is well known locally and throughout Russia, rather like the expression 'to drink like a fish' in English.

Iremashvili went on: *Terrible and undeserved beatings made the boy as rough, unsociable and heartless as his father, and bred a hostility in him towards anybody who tried to exercise authority over him.* Stalin's daughter, Svetlana, who left Russia for the West with de-Stalinisation and wrote a juicy biography, relates that her father told her how one day, in defence of his mother: *He threw a knife at old Vissarion. His father chased after him shouting like a madman and the neighbours had to hide the child.*

And the last straw would have been the 'abduction of a sort', as it would be termed by present-day justice, when Iosif's father snatched his son away from his studies to work as an apprentice in the shoe factory, against the wishes of his wife, who had struggled to get a grant for Iosif so that he could continue his religious studies. The details of this clash over the boy's education are unknown, but as we have related here, one thing that is clear is that ultimately the boy's self-sacrificing mother won through.

CHAPTER II

THE SEMINARY AT TIFLIS

In August, Keke took her son to be enrolled at the seminary in Tiflis. The town and its lively streets made a great impression on Iosif, after the small village where he had spent his childhood.

On 1st September, he enrolled as a boarder at the seminary, where he was to remain for almost the next six years, unaware that the religious establishment, like many others scattered around Russia, was a centre for nationalist unrest.

At that time, the workers were tired of the absolutist power of Nicolas II, who was a weak man and a puppet controlled by his wife, the Tsarina Alexandra Feodorovna. She in turn was a pawn in the hands of one of the most influential members of Court, the 'staretz' (self-styled holy man) Rasputin. Unrest was stirred up at secret meetings, almost always spurred on by two men, Plekhanov and Axelrod, who were the pioneers of the secret group Land and Freedom. Although these men were against violence and terrorism, they considered that the Marxism they advocated was the concern of the workers and not of the Russian peasants.

The secret meetings and the bad conditions that reigned amongst the working class obliged the Tsar to impose stronger methods of repression, carried out by the Okhrana, the Imperial secret police, and he invested large amounts of money in the infiltration of his spies wherever the workers were likely to meet, so that a great number of people were forced to flee into exile to Germany, Switzerland or France under threat of being imprisoned and forgotten in the imperial dungeons.

Plekhanov fled to France, where in Paris, in 1889, he made contact with the Second International.

In 1898, the socialist leaders met in Minsk, in an attempt to unify all the Marxist groups. The result was an agreement to form a single party under the name of Russian Social-Democrats. The party was clandestine, but gathered huge numbers of followers, and slowly but surely the group incorporated other revolutionary groups. The exception was the Narodnik Party, which defended the theory that it was up to the Russian peasants to pioneer the change from the prevailing feudalism to a much sought-after socialism.

However, Plekhanov's party was much better organised, controlling important secret networks all over Russia and even in Western Europe. They published the newspaper *Iskra*, and in their numerous clandestine press offices throughout the country leaflets and even books, which they distributed secretly.

This organisation was of course involved in a constant battle with the state police, but even so it found its way into universities, factories, and finally, into the seminary in Tiflis.

Conflicts in the seminary

By the time the young Iosif Dzhugashvili entered the seminary it was already a centre of unrest, and several students had previously been expelled for their revolutionary ideas. In 1886, reaching extremes, the archpriest Tchudnietski had been murdered by one of the students. There were riotous uprisings in the classrooms, and a year before Iosif enrolled, a student strike in protest of the fact that all the monks teaching at the school were Russian had forced the school to remain closed for some months.

As a result of all this, by the time Iosif arrived the establishment was ruled with an iron, almost military, discipline. The students rose at seven in the morning, and the entire day was devoted to prayers, classes, and more prayers, except for two hours after the main meal. Wardrobes and suitcases were continually searched on the lookout for evidence of subversion. Stalin was later to write about his time in the school:

> *It was then that I became a socialist, because I could not bear the strict discipline that was imposed at the school. It was crawling with spies. We would have tea at nine o'clock, and afterwards when we went to bed we would find that all our wardrobes and belongings in the bedrooms had been searched. And in the same way as they daily ransacked our possessions, they scrutinised our souls. It was unbearable.*

Stalin's first months in the seminary were more or less uneventful. He was considered a good student by his teachers, studious and disciplined, a view which contrasted with his true introverted self. But his strength of character was soon to show itself amongst his schoolmates, as it had in Gori. He always wanted to be the leader and the first in everything, especially in games. He told his friends to call him by the name of 'Koba' (the Dread). He started to become involved in plots and conspiracies, with students older than himself, and it was then that he first heard talk of Marx, Engels and socialism.

He found these theories very interesting, and whenever he was allowed out of the seminary he would go to the town library, and flagrantly ignoring the rules of the monks at school, he would read whatever literature he could get his hands on, from Balzac's *Human Comedy* to *Das Kapital* by Marx, which was passed around secretly from hand to hand.

However, it was not until his third year at Tiflis that Koba joined the seminar's clandestine socialist circle, although he always wanted to be the leader. By that time he had lost his religious faith almost totally and was a believer in Darwinism.

In this period the monks at the seminary also began to understand the true personality of one of their best pupils, and Iosif's name started to appear regularly in the punishment record:

> *Dzhugashvili has a card for the town library, which he uses to take books out* - is written in a note. *Today we have found* Toilers of the Sea, *by Victor Hugo, in his possession.*

And the punishments became more and more severe:

> *That he be locked up in the punishment cell for a long time. I have warned him about a banned book,* Ninety-Three, *by Victor Hugo.*

However, these punishments had no effect on the behaviour of the young Iosif, and meanwhile, in Tiflis the first railway strike was declared, marking the point at which Marx's class struggle came to prevail over nationalism, and the point at which the revolutionist group of the seminary went into action. Koba, at seventeen, was named as political director of a group of rail workers. He had to sneak out of the seminary after curfew for a meeting at a large house in the district with workers whom he instructed on the principals of socialism.

The following August, Iosif Dzhugashvili became a member of the Third Group, a movement of revolutionary intellectuals founded in 1893 by the writer Ninochvili, editor of the most influential newspaper in Georgia, the *Kvali*.

CHAPTER III

ABANDONING THE SEMINARY

In the 1898-99 academic year, Koba, completely uninterested in his studies, with his religious beliefs lost definitively, and making fun of the monks and of prayer, decided to leave the seminary.

By the time of his departure, Stalin had turned into a true socialist.

Tiflis had strengthened his will-power, increasing his aversion to established authority and turning him into a true revolutionary.

In the autumn of 1899, Koba was again to be found in Gori. There he became tutor of an Armenian, Simon Ter-Petrosian, a young man expelled from school for causing grave offence to religion.

But soon, unable to bear that placid occupation for long, he returned suddenly to Tiflis where he continued to frequent the clandestine places where the socialist workers met.

Without a stable occupation, it was his friends who made collections to support his needs, since Keke, in spite of all her efforts, could hardly help him.

Finally, at the end of 1899, he found a job as assistant in the Tiflis Observatory. The salary was not much, but the advantages for Stalin were obvious. In the first place, he had a room available for his exclusive use, and the work was not overwhelming, so he could meet with many of his party comrades in his room; this saved him to a certain extent from police inquiries.

In fact, in the last months, numerous members of the party had been arrested by the Okhrana*. From that moment on, Stalin lived like a clandestine militant, using his well demonstrated qualities of deception, prudence and presence of mind.

In these clandestine meetings in the room at the Observatory, the first manifesto in the Caucasus of 1st May was prepared at the instigation of Josep Djugachvili.

On that date, some hundreds of the city's workers met on the banks of Lake Salago, later marching in file, waving red flags, portraits of Marx and Engels and singing the *Marseilleise*. Koba gave the first public political speech of his life there.

In the following year, Koba decided to repeat the demonstration, but this year it took place in the very centre of Tiflis. A little before, a friend of Lenin, Victor Kurnatovsky, had arrived in Tiflis; he produced a strong impression on Koba and his comrades, to whom he spoke about Lenin's ideas. For his part, Kurnatovsky received a very good impression of the young man employed at the Observatory, whom he considered one of the leading revolutionaries in Georgia.

For the expected demonstration, leaflets were distributed which declared that "the whips and sabres of the police do not intimidate us." But, to counter this daring demonstration, the Okhrana made a large-scale raid a little before the day announced for the demonstration – 1st May – arresting and imprisoning Kurnatovsky and the majority of the local leaders. But when the police burst into Koba's room in the Observatory, the future Stalin had disappeared...

---

* The secret Tsarist police; the KGB of the 'old regime'.

Stalin's mother was completely devoted to her son's education.

Naturally, Joseph was not able to return to his occupation, and in future had to live underground, adopting an infinite number of names to escape police persecution.

In spite of this adversity, Koba did not abandon his idea of organising the demonstration already planned. Without much help, certainly, he carried on with a sense of conviction, meeting with the groups, changing his hiding-place from day to day, and editing leaflets signed with distinguished names.

The result of all this was that on the planned date, almost 3,000 workers gathered in Soldatsky Bazar, near the garden of Alexander, right in the centre of Tiflis.

The workers were expected by the police and the Cossacks. The clash was bloody, producing a great number of wounded, and many of the demonstrators were arrested, although Stalin was not among them – he was able to make a lucky escape.

Afterwards he spent some time in Gori, deciding to return to Tiflis once things had calmed down. There the socialist committee was reorganised and he became a member, behaving in future like a true leader; particularly when, from Leipzig, the newspaper *Iskra* (The Spark) - whose director was Lenin himself - had been published , referring to the events of 1st May:

> *"What occurred in Tiflis has a historic importance for the whole of the Caucasus. The revolutionary movement has been openly instituted in the Caucasus!"*

In spite of all this, the strong personality of Djibladze at first imposed itself on the Committee; he was a member of the more moderate wing, opposed to hostile demonstrations and agitators; Koba, in contrast, was a fervent supporter of them.

In a short time, Joseph Djugachvili tried to discredit Djibladze by means of devious manoeuvres, in such a way that finally Joseph was made to appear before a commission, which decided to exclude him from the Committee and even ordered him to leave the city.

At the end of November, Stalin went to Batum, making contact with the socialists there, to whom he gave his own version of his departure from Tiflis.

In the first days of February 1902 a strike was declared at the Mantachev factory, achieving a number of demands. But another later strike, this time at the Rothschild factory, was violently repressed by the police at the request of the factory management, and four hundred workers were arrested or imprisoned.

In response, on 9th March, six thousand male and female unarmed workers marched on the prison where their comrades were imprisoned to demand their freedom. The outcome was bloody; fourteen dead and more than forty injured, as well as fifty more arrested.

Koba made an impact in that demonstration, putting himself forward as its organiser. But some members of the Batum Committee accused Djugachvili of having double-crossed them: on the one hand, slowing down the "march", while knowing, on the other, that the police were going to prove remorseless.

Koba's situation was delicate when, suddenly, he was arrested by the Okhrana. The most widely spread rumour was that the police had acted in this way rather to protect him.

The situation in the country was alarming. The Russian Empire appeared to be large and powerful. It extended across an immense territory of almost 237 million square feet (practically the same as the modern USSR) and had a population of approximately 170 million inhabitants. But this strength was not real because the economic and social structure reflected a very great imbalance between an archaic rural, Russia which was numerically very important, and a very localised, minority part of the Empire which was becoming industrialised very quickly, with all the problems of a working class which was all the time more active, open to all the doctrines of redemption that had then been invented: utopian socialism, anarchism, Marxism.

What did Tsarism count on to defend its position in the face of the revolutionary tide, whose waves had already mortally wounded some of its representatives: Alexander II, Alexander III...? It counted on a *bureaucracy* that was numerous enough to be able to oversee such an extensive empire, and also corrupt - its officials had turned into a true administrative nobility. On an *army* whose positions of command were exclusively reserved for the nobility. On the *Orthodox Church* (a version of Christianity with Greco-Byzantine rather than Roman origins: the Church was separated from Constantinople by Peter I the Great at the end of the 17th century and beginning of the 18th). It held a great influence over the illiterate masses (some 80% of the population) and exercised a role of guardian of order and tradition – its head was the Tsar himself. And finally, on the *Okhrana*, the key participant in a repressive system that was of such strength that it was able to maintain order.

Demonstrations and confrontations were frequent, but although many victims had now been claimed, they were still street-level outbursts, isolated plots against royalty or the nobility. The authentic revolution had still not reached its maturity.

CHAPTER IV

FIRST UPRISINGS

Koba spent 18 months in jail, first in Batum, then moving on to Kutans and finally returning to Batum prison.

During these 18 months the Russian workers' movement was becoming organised.

The socialist revolutionaries, who had succeeded the popular movement, created the Socialist-Revolutionary Party. For their part, the liberals formed "The Emancipation". The Social-Democrat and Socialist-Revolutionary Committees also merged.

In 1902, specifically in the month of March, Lenin's book *What is to be done?* was published; in this, from his exile in Europe, he posed the question whether it was appropriate to create a party restricted to revolutionaries or, to the contrary, a party which was broad and open to all. Lenin advocated the first of these alternatives.

At the beginning of 1903, the daily newspaper *Iskra*, which was clandestinely introduced into Russia from abroad, announced the Second Congress of the POSDR – the Russian Social Democratic Workers Party – which was due to be held in Brussels from 17th July to 10th August in that same year.

The organization of the Congress provoked confrontations between Lenin and Plekhanov. Trotsky and Martov supported Lenin and he, influenced by the ideas of his collaborators, described the position of Plekhanov as only valid for a political manual.

Nevertheless, it was the position of Plekhanov which prevailed as the basis for discussion in the Congress. To begin with this took place in Brussels, and afterwards, owing to problems which had arisen with the Belgian police, in a church in London – the city where Lenin was living. During the course of the Congress, Lenin had to confront a split within his own group: on the one side, there formed a faction, led by Plekhanov and Lenin, which gained the name *bolche* - more votes – and on the other one headed by Martov, which gained the name *menche* – less votes.

Lenin was unable to prevent the Bolshevik – Menshevik split.

Trotsky, for his part, supported Martov, since he saw in Lenin a despot and a terrorist.

Lenin went through a depressive phase because of the Congress, although he soon enough recovered his energies to defend his position in favour of the union of the peasants in opposition to the 'Menshevik' position, which supported union with the liberal bourgeoisie.

Koba himself supported the Mensheviks' thesis during that period, at least as described in a later Russian police report, in which Joseph Djugachvili is described as a sinister person with a 'pock-marked face', the effect of the small-pox which he suffered in Gori in his childhood.

In November 1903, Koba was deported to Novaia Uda, a small village in southern Siberia near to its capital, Irkutsk.

It is not known for sure when Koba escaped, whether during his transfer to Novaia Uda or in the few weeks of his forced exile in that region, but it is certain that in January 1904 Stalin had returned to Batum.

From that city, Koba took himself to Tiflis, where he married Catalina Svanidze. The wedding was religious, since Catalina, who was very devout, demanded this of Koba.

During this period, Koba was not at all decided which party to choose, the Bolsheviks or Mencheviks, although it is possible that during that time he may have already decided in favour of Bolshevism.

Towards the end of 1904, an oilfield workers' strike was declared in Baku. Chendrikov, one of the Menshevik leaders, took charge of the movement. Koba, despite the fact that he arrived in the city after the start of the strike, took no part in the demonstration. But with their protest the workers succeeded in obtaining the collective bargaining meeting to negotiate pay and conditions, which led to a nine-hour day by rotation of three teams.

Bloody Sunday

In one year, owing to the Russo-Japanese war, the forces of the Tsar suffered serious defeats; the fleet, brought over from Europe, was destroyed on 26th May 1905. The crushing military defeat brought disastrous consequences.

During the course of 1905, Russia lost more than 500,000 million roubles, and thousands of men died not only because of the war, but also from hunger and epidemics.

The Baku strike came immediately before the famous Bloody Sunday.

On Sunday, 9th January 1905, a mass of workers, headed by the priest Father Gapon, began a march on the Winter Palace, in St. Petersburg, to present a petition to the Tsar.

The demonstrators, convinced that the Tsar would provide a solution to their misfortunes, brought their portraits and icons with them as a display of affection to their "little father".

But the palace guards charged against the crowd, causing hundreds of deaths. This charge was the beginning of the revolution.

Taking refuge in Finland, Father Gapon wrote to the Tsar in these hard terms:

> *The innocent blood of the workers, of their wives and children, will always lie between you, destroyer of souls! and the Russian people. A moral bond will now never be possible between you and them. May all the blood which you have shed, executioner, fall on you and your descendants...!*

The strikes spread throughout Russia and from February the revolt crossed over its borders. There were uprisings in Poland and in various cities the workers elected Committees, models for the future Soviets.

The Tsar, realising that he was forced to concede, promised to hold a constitutional assembly, a 'Duma', although he refused to allow the workers' representatives to take part in it; this provoked protests through some of the opposition parties.

In October, a new general strike was declared.

In Saint Petersburg, the workers chose a Council of Deputies, presided over by Trotsky, and for some time this Soviet actually took over the reins of power, since the people obeyed its orders and rejected those of the Emperor.

But the Okhrana took charge of arresting all the members of the Soviet, which brought with it an intensification of the revolts and an increase in strikes in consequence, culminating in December in the Moscow uprising.

Nevertheless, workers and peasants would have to wait another 12 years before they could again rise up against the Tsarist regime of Nicholas II.

During that crucial year of 1905, Koba adopted his final position: he would support the Bolshevik theses.

During that year, his son Yasha was born.

CHAPTER V

MEETING WITH LENIN

On 8th November of the same year, Lenin arrived at Saint Petersburg from Geneva. It had been decided that the Fourth Congress of the POSDR should take place in the Russian capital.

The date was fixed for 10th December, but in the face of the tight surveillance which the Okhrana maintained over Lenin, it was finally decided that the Congress would be held at Tammersfors, in Finland.

The POSD of the Caucasus region had to send three delegates, and Koba took advantage of the occasion to get himself named as delegate for Tiflis, although it is a mystery how he succeeded, given that the majority of the Caucasus Committee was made up of Mensheviks, who hated Djugachvili.

This was the first time that Joseph left the Caucasus using the name of Ivanovitch in his passport.

It was also his first meeting with Lenin, whom he described in the following way:

> *I had expected to see the eagle of the party, as much from a physical as a political point of view. I imagined Lenin as an imposing giant. How great my disappointment was to meet with such an ordinary man, of a smaller height than average, the same as so many other mortals...!*

I felt disappointed to see that Lenin had arrived at the conference before the other delegates, not as a man of importance who had to be waited for to emphasise his importance; and, in addition, he stood in a corner in the simplest way in the world, talking with the least known of the delegates.

Despite this first impression, he modified his opinion after Lenin's speeches. Of these he said:

The two speeches given by Lenin were important; one dealt with the political situation and the other with the agrarian question. He spoke inspirationally, arousing a wild enthusiasm in the room. His extraordinary power of persuasion, the simplicity and clarity of his arguments, his agile phrases, his lack of affectation – all these gave Lenin an undeniable superiority over the other usual speakers.

But, on the other hand, the Congress developed in a way which was not greatly to Joseph's liking, when he saw that in one of the day's motions there was to be an attempt at bringing the Bolsheviks and Mensheviks closer together. This motion, presented and defended by the delegate Lazovsky, proposing the merger of both organisations, was finally approved, without Koba being able to intervene.

In other words, from then on, Koba – who had until then fought against the Mensheviks, believing that he was following Lenin's directives - had to get on with them on his return to Tiflis.

Four months later the Reunification Conference met in Stockholm and, curiously, once again Joseph Dzugachvili was one of the eleven Tiflis delegates, of whom ten were Mensheviks.

Aged 17, when he escaped from the Seminary to pursue his political activities.

The boieviki

In the Stockholm conference, Koba openly opposed Lenin concerning the distribution of land. Lenin was a supporter of the nationalisation of land belonging to the nobility, pure and simple. A good number of delegates supported this idea, but Koba showed his disagreement and in his turn proposed to allow the peasants the right to appropriate the land they wanted, without more ado.

The conference finally voted against the expropriations – that is, armed robberies by the *boieviki*, Bolshevik bandits carrying out raids to help party funds. Although Lenin allied himself with this vote, in his own mind it mattered little where the money came from which he needed to support his print shops, his newspapers and to help his comrades in exile.

The *boieviki*, with whom Koba would in future find himself mixed up in armed raid, carried out more than a thousand terrorist attacks in the Caucasus alone in just four years. They were led by the Bolshevik Kote Tsintsadze, to 'expropriate the funds of the Imperial Treasury.'

In 1907, Joseph Djugachvili was called urgently to Batum, where his wife Catalina Svanidze was dying. She died in April 1907, after receiving the last rites.

The afore-mentioned Ian Grey states that Stalin probably suffered greatly from the death of his young wife, but the description of Iremachvili of his theatrical behaviour at the funeral is hardly convincing: *At the gates of the cemetery, Koba squeezed my hand tightly, pointed to the coffin and said: "This child softened my heart of stone! She has died, and with her, my feelings of affection to any human being!" He put his right hand against his heart: "I am profoundly desolated, indescribably desolated!"* This biographer states that the wedding took place in 1903. Ian Grey points out that Joseph was then in prison, but the Tsarist authorities, to demonstrate their closeness to the clergy, 'the alliance of the throne and the altar', of such fatal consequences for every kind of church, allowed the priests to conduct solemn weddings in prison.

Iremachvili writes that Ekaterina, his friend's wife, died in 1907, but Yasha, the son of both of them, was born in 1908, according to Ian Grey, who relies on the evidence of Ekaterina's sisters, so this biographer concludes: *the death of Stalin's wife probably did not take place until 1910*. Be that as it may, what is certain is that the death of his young wife caused the future dictator's character, already deformed by his father, to become desensitised. Relentless towards himself, he became relentless towards everyone else. Yasha, in time, would eventually rise to the rank of general in the Red Army.

Joseph never spoke about this marriage because he believed that true revolutionaries should consider these matters to be personal, adding to this his own introversion and reserve about his private life. Having recently left the seminary, he probably felt some affection for her, but in his heart he had to fight against the tender reproaches she would made when he returned home after clandestine meetings or violent acts that he should abandon everything which could displease the Lord and leave the life of constant action and shocks for another more peaceful one, dedicated to monotonous daily work and to his selfless wife and son.

Without her presence and support, Stalin embraced forever the hazardous career of the professional revolutionary, which gave him the unique opportunity to bring to the surface the reserves of hatred and resentment which he had been accumulating inside. His past experiences living in a seminary had prepared him magnificently for taking part in conspiracies and had taught him to suspect everyone; they helped to increase his shrewdness and gifts for deceit, his revolutionary practices, at the same time as his aversion and his envy towards authority were increased by the persecutions of the Tsarist secret police. He also assimilated the techniques of his persecutors, who resorted to inquisitorial proceedings to obtain 'confessions' - he learnt from them, in other words, everything that could be learnt about threats, physical violence, moral torture, falsification of confessions, bribery of false witnesses and other weapons in the arsenal of terror and oppression. He never forgot those lessons, and applied them with such mastery, when he was in power, that it would have embarrassed his own Tsarist persecutors.

CHAPTER VI

STALIN HAS TO TRAVEL

In the month of May, Stalin travelled to London together with six delegates from the Caucasus, to take part in the Fifth Congress of the POSDR, where for the first time he saw Trotsky.

Of this meeting, one of the delegates said:

> *He saw in London the man who, in the future, would be his most obstinate rival. He was of medium height, with a very pronounced profile and an aquiline nose. With a wide forehead, it appeared larger because he had his hair combed back. Large and sensual mouth. Koba asked me who he was and I told him the name: Trotsky, who was considered the best orator in the party, the author of the theory of permanent revolution.*

It was at this Congress where, during a debate on the question of the Party's financial difficulties, the idea arose – put forward by Krazzin, Lenin's right-hand man – of ransacking the Public Treasury of Tiflis, where there were always large sums of money.

The idea was approved unanimously and the man put in charge of putting it into action was one who, through his phlegmatic and decisive character, could be most trusted to make a success of the plan, particularly because of his knowledge of the city: Joseph Djugachvili.

He accepted, and 5,000 roubles were handed over to him for the preparation of the coup, as well as a passport in the name of David Chizhikov, native of Vladivostok.

The date of the raid was fixed for 13th June – the knowing Koba was aware that on this date a substantial sum of money would be transported. The convoy would be passing along Solokasnia Street and crossing Erivanskia Square.

Koba put Ter-Petrosian in charge of getting hold of arms and explosives.

The hold-up

On the appointed day, around ten in the morning, two horse-drawn carriages, with an escort of Cossacks, drew up in front of the Post Office building. The cashier and a clerk from the Bank of Tiflis dismounted from the first carriage and from the second came two guards armed with rifles. At that moment, a woman who was watching the operation made her way to a nearby cafe from which she made a phone-call to a restaurant in Tilikuhhury Street, where Koba and his comrades selected for the raid were waiting.

Koba hurriedly left the restaurant and positioned himself on the roof of a building adjoining the Post Office, from where he could observe the progress of the operation.

When the employees of the Bank left the Post Office carrying some bags full of money, another woman, on the pavement, took out a handkerchief, the agreed signal for the attackers.

At this signal, a horse-drawn carriage in which a uniformed official – in actual fact, Ter-Petrosian – was travelling, approached the Post Office, at the same moment as a bomb, thrown from the roof where Koba was positioned, fell in the middle of the first carriages, creating a large explosion. To this first bomb were added various others thrown from the pavement, while some shots were fired. The Cossacks were unable to react in time and the cashier and clerk of the Bank lay on the road seriously injured. Then, the official - Ter-Petrosian – got out of the carriage which had been slowly approaching, took possession of the bags, got back into the carriage again and escaped, firing his pistol.

The whole incident lasted no more than a few minutes. The police were unable to discover any clues, since the raid had been carried out with great precision.

Koba and his comrades had taken possession of 340,000 roubles in notes, Treasury bills and Railway Company shares.

Nevertheless, this acquisition of money brought the Bolsheviks a bad reputation.

The booty was clandestinely sent to Finland, where Lenin lived at that time; he put comrade Litvinov in charge of changing the proceeds of the robbery in Paris. But he fell into the hands of the police and the whole affair ended in disaster.

In the meantime, Koba, in his new name of Chighikov, settled in Baku, where the Bolsheviks were powerful, and was there elected member of the city's Oil Committee.

Of this episode in his life, Stalin said:

> *Two years of revolutions among the oil workers, in Baku, hardened me as a fighter and turned me into a leading activist. There I learnt for the first time what it means to lead great masses of workers.*

Because of these events, the counter-revolution of the Stolypin Government began to act with great efficiency, and the 'deliveries' to Siberia multiplied.

At the Party's Fifth Congress, held in London, Koba explained the growing difficulties which the agitators in Russia were facing. Nonetheless, on his return to Baku, Joseph took up his revolutionary activities again, surrounded by people who would soon come to figure in a significant way in the Party: Vorochilov, Spandarian, Chaumian, and others.

As president of the Council of Government, Piotr Stolypin had succeeded the conservative Goriemskin, who was a scheming and reactionary old man, a true puppet who undid whatever good had been achieved by the loyal and tireless Witte – the man who had been left to "carry the can" and sign the humiliation before Japan.

On 11th April 1906, Father Georgui Gapon, leader of the demonstration in front of the Winter Palace on 'Bloody Sunday' in January 1905, was assassinated by the revolutionary socialists, who believed him to be an *agent provocateur*. His treachery was to write to Durnovo, the Interior Minister, offering him his services.

Stolypin was a natural and unscrupulous politician who committed two fundamental errors: his agrarian law, which created a new wretched and desperate class, the rural proletariat; and his incredible attempt at the violent Russification of the country, imposing all kinds of taxes on the national minorities. In his Government he satisfied no one. In spite of the apparent pacification, terrorism reached unimaginable extremes; there were months in which three hundred civil or military officials were assassinated. He governed using every kind of terror; the gallows were called 'Stolypin's tie'. One of his collaborators described him thus: "His high stature, his frosty voice, everything about his look showed a dominant, unfeeling and cruel nature" (much like Stalin's!).

On 25th August 1906, he was the target of a daring bomb attack. It caused 27 victims, among them two sons of the President who were wounded. The bomb exploded in his office and Stolypin only received some spatterings of ink. On 14th September 1911, the attack proved fatal.

It happened in the theatre of Kiev and was perpetrated by Dimitri Bogrov, a lawyer by profession with anarchist ideas. He succeeded in entering the theatre thanks to a pass which the chief of the secret police in Kiev, Kuliabko, had given him on passing himself off as an informer. Kuliabko made his entry into the theatre possible so that he could help him detect the possible presence of anarchists. Taking advantage of this situation, Bogrov was able to approach the Prime Minister, next to the orchestra, and shoot him in the head before the curtain was raised.

The author of the attack was immediately arrested and given a most trial, at which he was sentenced to death. With the death of Stolypin, tsarism's last political figure with a strong personality disappeared from the scene.

The last politicians were a sorry bunch. In fact, they came to power on the recommendation of the mysterious and loathsome Rasputin. None of them would have the talent and the energy necessary to save the country.

CHAPTER VII

NEW EXILE

Again in the hands of the Okhrana

In the face of the dangerous turn which these events were taking for his personal security, Koba changed his last name to that of Organus Totmyants, although this did not prevent him being detained together with other comrades.

Of his arrest, it is recorded in the Police report:

> *A very dangerous man. He is a leader of the highest category, although there does not exist much evidence against him.*

This report was sent, nonetheless, to the Ministry of Internal Affairs.

Joseph Djugachvili was on this occasion sentenced to two years' exile on his own in Vologda in Siberia.

He did not spend long in this place, since he soon obtained a new passport in the name, this time, of Muradians, and on 24th June 1908 left for Moscow, and from there returned to Baku.

Shortly afterwards he was again arrested and after spending half a year in prison he was deported yet again to Siberia, where he stayed until the year 1911.

Once free, he made for Saint Petersburg, and wrote numerous letters, again under the pseudonym of Koba, which he sent to the Party newspapers abroad. They were published under the title of *Correspondence from St. Petersburg*, and in them he showed himself a fervent supporter of Lenin, attacking the Mensheviks.

Lenin echoed these letters in an article published in *The Social-Democrat*, in these terms:

> *The correspondence of comrade Koba deserves our total attention... It is hard to think of a more appropriate rebuttal of the concepts of the 'reconciliators' – he was referring to the moderate socialists. Of Trotsky, in the same article, he said: 'Anyone who supports Trotsky's group supports the politics of deception of the workers, which helps the pretence of the 'liquidators'.*

Once again, Koba was recognised in St. Petersburg and put into prison in September 1911. A little later he was sent to Vologda, this time for three years.

At the beginning of 1912, Koba was visited by Sergio Ordjonikidze, who brought some good news: in that very month of January, a conference had taken place in Prague and the Bolshevik faction had chosen a new central committee, in which – in the second vote, although not in the first – Lenin had succeeded in having Koba chosen as one of the five leaders.

It was the first time that Lenin had interceded on behalf of Koba, who then decided to leave his forced residence, departing on 29th February for St. Petersburg.

After a short journey to visit Koba in order to rebuild a Bolshevik committee, he returned to St Petersburg, taking part there in the translation of the newspaper *Zverzda* and the launch of *Pravda*, whose first edition went out on 22nd April 1912, with an editorial signed by him, where he said:

In the year 1905, Joseph Vissarionovitch decided to support the Bolshevik theses.

*We believe that a strong and vigorous movement
is unthinkable without there being argument. A total
conformity of viewpoints cannot lead to anything
other than disaster.*

*In fact, what Koba was seeking was final union with the
Mensheviks.*

On the same day on which the future official newspaper
of Soviet Russia appeared, Koba was again arrested, sent to
prison and subsequently sentenced to three years' exile in the
Narym region, in Western Siberia.

He spent little time in this place, since in the month of
September of the same year, 1912, he returned to St. Petersburg
where, with a comrade of the Party, a student called Vyachesalv
Mikhailovich Skryabin – alias Molotov, he assured the continuation of *Pravda*.

There were a good many articles by Lenin published in the
newspaper, but on a number of occasions they also forgot to
send the money to Lenin for his contributions.

Lenin ended up becoming angry and called Koba to
Warsaw, and after telling him what he thought of *Pravda*,
sent for Sverdlov to put him in charge of the newspaper.

On 12th January 1913, an article appeared for the first time
in the newspaper signed by J. Stalin, the name which Lenin
himself, after discussion and later reconciliation with Koba,
advised him to adopt.

Days later, Stalin left for Vienna, where he had to carry
out a study opposing the cultural autonomy of the nationalist Austrian minorities, and also opposing the Jewish socialist position and the federalism of Georgia's Mensheviks.

In Vienna, Stalin met Trotsky again, and this time it was
Trotsky who described the Georgian:

A man with a tender look, a sad gaze, an aggressive manner, who expresses himself in grunts...

From Vienna, Stalin proceeded to Krakow where he wrote *Marxism and the national question*, the most valuable theoretical work of those which he wrote, perhaps because the style was not his, but more closely reflects the Leninist influence.

Stalin then returned to St Petersburg; on 23rd February 1914, while he was attending a concert, the police, tipped off by an informer, made a rapid strike against him. Although Stalin covered himself with a cape lent to him by the wife of the orchestral director, a friend of his, a policeman approached him and, lifting up his hood, recognised him.

This time he was sentenced to four years' exile at Turukhansk, near the Arctic circle. It was the place reserved for the most dangerous revolutionaries. The Okhrana, finally, recognised the 'merits' of Stalin.

Svetlana, Stalin's daughter, wrote that her father referred at times to Siberia, speaking of "its severe beauty and its silent and unrefined people." He got on well with its inhabitants, who taught him to fish in the River Yenisei, but – instead of remaining in one place, as they did – he went from one side to the other until he discovered a place in which the fishes took the bait well. The quantity of fish which he caught was often so great that the Siberians came to the conclusion that Stalin had supernatural powers and told him: *You know the secret.*

One day, a terrible snow storm broke in mid-winter; Stalin was returning to the village when he got lost. He then approached two peasants and saw with amazement how they hurried away from him at great speed. He later found out that his face was so covered with snow and ice that he had the appearance of a ghost. His daughter revealed years later that some aunts of hers had said that in that period of forced exile he had lived with a local woman with whom he had a son. As the son had little education, he never sought to obtain a surname.

In Siberia, Stalin grew bored. His forced inactivity contributed to the disintegration of the Bolshevik organisation. The circulation of *Pravda* fell from 40,000 copies to half that, because of the split in the Duma (Parliament) between the Bolsheviks and more moderate Mensheviks. At the same time, the secret police carried on arresting all the Bolshevik activists and depriving the party of its leadership.

CHAPTER VIII

THE EUROPEAN WAR

In August 1914 the European War broke out and the Russians found themselves confronted with Germany. The Russians' method of fighting was very simple: to crush the enemy under their mass, with bayonet attacks; the Germans responded to this with machine-guns and cannons, causing heavy Russian losses in the battlefields.

In the Court, the losses caused discomfort and factions developed, each blaming the others for the disasters of the front. The Tzarina followed the advice of Rasputin, which made the hatred which the people felt for the foreigner grow.

Trotsky wrote, in relation to this:

> *To justify this situation, this German woman, with a kind of calculated anger, adopted the traditions and manners of Russian feudalism, the most despicable and vulgar type of all, and this at a time when the people were exerting their greatest efforts to free themselves from it. This Princess of Hesse has been possessed by the demon of autocracy.*

There were, in total, 15 million men conscripted by the army, which was under the command of Sukhomlinov.

But in spite of everything, the Russian people, thwarting the revolutionary leaders, did not rise up against the Tsar; on the contrary, now that all the strikes had been suppressed, the workers started up their work again and proclaimed their loyalty to the Tsar, who declared that he would never sign a peace treaty while a single German soldier remained on Russian soil.

Meanwhile, Stalin, in exile, finished the *Study of the Nationalities,* whose manuscript he sent to Lenin; Lenin, in turn, delivered his *Manifesto to the Party* and *The Working Class* to him from Switzerland.

The ideas put across in this *Manifesto* created violent debates among the exiles, since the majority of them were opposed to Lenin's point of view.

Nonetheless, Stalin was in agreement with him, since he considered that violence was the only means of fighting against power.

The war continued to be bloody, with disasters and misery. Rasputin was hated more every day until finally, during the night of 29th to 30th December 1916, he was assassinated by Prince Yussupoff and a number of his friends.

The death of the hated *staretz* was received with joy across Russia and soon in Petrograd – the new name imposed on St. Petersburg, which had too strong a German connotation - three centres of agitation were established: the Union of the Peoples, an organisation of aristocratic outlook, which simply wanted a change in the Palace; the extreme left and the social democrats. These last tried, through the organisation 'Mezhrayonka', to unite the Bolsheviks and Mensheviks. Trotsky formed part of the assembly, as did Maximo Gorki.

CHAPTER IX

FEBRUARY, PRELUDE TO THE OCTOBER REVOLUTION

On 18th February 1917, when food was now very scarce and there was no fuel for heating, the first workers' demonstrations occurred in the textile sector; they continued until the 23rd, when the strike extended to other factories, concluding finally on the 25th with a general strike.

The police confronted the demonstrations, causing the first outcries, and shots were fired on both sides, with dead and injured.

On the 27th, the workers, supported this time by guards, attacked the police stations of the Okhrana. Their arsenal was looted and the Palace of Justice set on fire.

The Duma, the legislative assembly instituted by Nicholas II after the revolution of 1905, was supposed to open its sessions on 27th February. On the 28th, delegates from the workers' party formed an executive Committee of Soviets, and for their part the deputies on the left formed a provisional Committee.

Kerensky made a virulent speech of accusation against the Government, demanding an end to the war.

On 1st March, bread was rationed and the bakeries were raided.

In an effort to impose a degree of order on the prevailing chaos caused by the fact that the Tsar – at that time more than

300 miles away from Petrograd – did not react, preferring to believe the news which arrived from the Winter Palace, from where the tsarina sent him a telegram telling him that "calm reigns in the city", on 2nd March the Duma named a provisional government led by Prince Lvov, of which Kerensky was a member.

But at the same time the Soviet published a decree in which it stated:

> *In all their public acts the military units are under the orders of the Soviet of workers' deputies and their committees. The orders stemming from the military Commission of the Duma shall be obeyed if they do not contradict the decisions taken by the Soviet.*

This dual position of command represented a clear confrontation between the bourgeois government and the revolutionaries, which would ultimately result in civil war.

Meanwhile, Stalin remained in exile, at that time in Krasnoyarsk, to where he had been transferred, but for a short time. Under the order of the Soviet of the capital the deportees were freed and on 12th March Stalin and his companions in exile arrived by train in Petrograd. On the same day, the Central Committee readmitted the Georgian leader, although only in a consultative role.

But Stalin was not a man to remain in the background, and a few days later he was already a full member of the Committee, chosen by the Presidium and designated, together with Kamenev, to represent the bureau before the Soviet Central Committee. At the same time, the newspaper *Pravda* came under the direction of Kamenev, Muranov and Stalin himself.

During this period, the paper published an editorial in which it recommended support for the provisional Government to fight against reaction and counter-revolution, inviting the contenders to sign a peace deal.

This stance annoyed the hard-line Bolsheviks who asked for the dismissal of the three deportees.

At the Party conference held on 27th March in Petrograd, Stalin defended himself with these words:

> *Power, when divided between two organs, is not exercised in full. There are frictions and struggles. The Soviet has taken the initiative in these revolutionary transformations and the provisional Government exercises the role of consolidator of the conquests of the revolutionary people. The Soviet mobilises its forces and controls them; the provisional Government wants to reaffirm the conquests of the people when they have already been achieved.*

Lenin opposed to Stalin

Lenin arrived at the Russian-Finnish frontier on 3rd April, coming from Switzerland. Kamenev received him and was insulted by the newcomer, who branded not only him, but also Muranov and Stalin as mad and reproached them for what had been published in *Pravda*.

In Petrograd, where he was received triumphantly by the Soviet delegation, Lenin advocated the victory of the socialist revolution; this represented a formal condemnation of Stalin's theories.

In the subsequent conference, before the meeting of the Bolsheviks and Mensheviks, he was booed when he declared that unity with the Mensheviks was really a betrayal of socialism.

> *We must take the initiative and create an interna-*
> *tional revolution! And it is better to be alone than to*
> *join up with the Mensheviks!*

This thesis, known as the *April Thesis*, was never finally adopted by the conference or by the Central Committee. Stalin, nonetheless, did not actually declare himself publicly against Lenin and maintained this position until the day on which he became the dictator of Russia.

In this regard, Trotsky said:

> *For Stalin, to be unnoticed at decisive moments*
> *and to change position in silence is becoming his*
> *most fundamental rule of conduct.*

Trotsky himself, at that time president of the Soviet of Petrograd, together with Zinoviev and several others, fired up the massed workers and the soldiers with enthusiasm, organising a demonstration for 10th June. But the Central Committee opposed this, organising its own demonstration for the 18th. That day, more than 500,000 people marched through the streets with placards demanding power for the Soviets and the fall of the capitalist ministers.

This demonstration was repeated on 3rd July, but in contrast to the earlier one, which did not lead to any violence, in this one the Government ordered the intervention of loyal troops and there were numerous casualties suffered by the workers in the face of their attack.

The print works where the newspaper *Pravda* was printed was also looted.

Lenin had to take refuge in the house of Sergio Alliluiev, leaving there shortly afterwards for Finland, under the protection of a disguise.

Trotsky, however, allowed himself to be arrested in order to assume responsibility, and was later freed on bail.

In the October Revolution of 1907, he was a member of the People's Commissars.

Lenin's desertion and Trotsky's forced renunciation conferred power on Stalin, who thus became the Bolshevik leader, although, faithful to his usual way of operating, he soon disappeared from the scene and spent many evenings in the house of Alliluiev, whose 17-year-old daughter was in love with the Georgian. Stalin, 21 years older than Nadejda, as the girl was called, married her in May 1919.

CHAPTER X

THE CIVIL WAR

The following weeks were tense and hectic. Supplies were growing scarcer all the time, and the peasants were taking possession of the lands that had been promised them. For their part, the Soviets refused to obey the Government.

From his exile in Finland, in October 1917, Lenin urged the Central Committee into action, while in Petrograd, Trotsky prepared the uprising, arming the Red Guards and preventing the departure to the war front of regiments loyal to the Bolsheviks.

Lenin put a Committee formed of seven members in charge of preparing for the takeover of power. The Committee was formed of Lenin himself, Trotsky, Zinoviev, Kamenev, Sokolnikov, Bubnov and Stalin.

At the Second Congress of the Soviet, which took place in Petrograd, Lenin attended and was highly acclaimed; he proposed in his speech that the Government should not be composed of ministers but People's Commissars. The suggestion was approved enthusiastically and Lenin was named President of the Council. Trotsky was put in charge of Foreign Affairs and Stalin of Nationalities.

The fall of the Winter Palace

During the following days, rumours took over the streets of the capital. It was claimed that Kerensky, at the head of troops loyal to the Government, was at the gates of Petrograd. Emboldened by this news, the cadets then occupied the telephone exchange, expelling the Red Guards, although this exchange changed hands several times in a few hours.

On 7th November, the Council of People's Commissars took the initiative, deciding to put an end once and for all to the confused situation. To do this, the Red Guards, under the orders of Antonoc-Ovssenko, positioned themselves around the Winter Palace.

At nine in the morning that day, two salvoes fired from the cruiser Aurora, whose crew was loyal to the Bolsheviks, opened the battle; it was immediately followed up by noisy rather than effective shelling of the Palace, although the battalion of women, who together with the cadets were in charge of its defence, surrendered. Finally, at dawn on the following day, the Government surrendered to the revolutionaries, although Kerensky was able to escape in a car supplied by the American Embassy.

Total power, at last, was in the hands of the Soviets, but the skirmishes did not cease yet and many confrontations took place in the streets of the city, although finally the insurgents, with Bujarin, Smirnov and Muralov at their head, prevailed.

Although the Council of People's Commissars issued many decrees - offering the belligerents a rapid peace, handing over lands to the peasants and abolishing the death penalty – and had a genuine desire for true democracy, it was not able to achieve this with as quickly as the socialists wanted, for the simple reason that, after so many years of oppression, the people were not ready suddenly to pass from mediaeval capitalism to socialism. For all that, Lenin thought that the most immediate measures, in principle, were to nationalise the Bank and to hand over control of production to the workers.

Contrary to what might have been expected, it was the peasants who were the first to rebel, protesting against the confiscations. Taking advantage of the situation, they were joined by all those who had suffered from the action of the Bolsheviks, in an attempt to overthrow Lenin, forming together – army officials, intellectuals, clergy, bourgeoisie – the so-called 'White Army', which brought about a real civil war that lasted four years and left Russia exhausted.

Meanwhile, the Soviets signed peace with Germany, although this did not come into effect immediately; the negotiations for the signing of the armistice, which should have been carried out in the Polish city of Brets-Litovsk by the two delegations, the German one headed by General Hoffmann and the Russian by Joffe, a friend of Trotsky's, broke down because of the heavy demands of the German's, who sought the hand-over of the whole of Poland and Lithuania and a large part of the Baltic States, which were inhabited by Ukrainians and dominated by the White Russians.

A new attempt at peace took place on 8th January 1918, this time with Trotsky at the head of the Russian delegation, and after some days of negotiations, the results were just as fruitless, since Trotsky, in the face of the repeated demands of the Germans, flatly refused to sign the armistice.

Days later the Germans renewed their offensive against Petrograd and Moscow.

This in the end brought about the resignation of Trotsky as Commissar for External Affairs, so as to take command of the Red Army, together with Skylansky, the leader of the Military Revolutionary Committee.

But the Council of Defence, of which Lenin, Trotsky himself, Krassin, Svedlov and Stalin were members, developed the political strategy.

Nevertheless, in the face of the German offensive, the Defence Committee decided finally to sign a peace agreement, Stalin being one of those who voted in favour of the resolution. And to achieve this agreement, Sokolnikov was sent to sign 'at any price'. The Germans had increased their demands, asking in addition for Finland and 300 million gold roubles.

Russia was thus deprived, in one blow, of a third of its population, of a large part of its crops and of almost half its industrial plants.

Meanwhile, the civil war continued. Stalin was sent to Tsaritsyn, an important strategic centre, which received petrol from the Caspian. There he plotted against Trotsky in such a way that Lenin had to be told of the situation by Trotsky himself, amazed at the anarchy which prevailed in the command. Then Stalin, in the face of the drastic actions taken by Trotsky, showed himself implacable against those who conspired against his authority, summarily executing spies and those who gave him the slightest suspicion.

Trotsky was himself shocked by the cruelty shown by Stalin and asked Lenin to reprimand him.

On the other fronts where there was fighting against the Whites, the Reds continued to achieve victories, working authentic miracles.

Stalin was sent to the Ukraine, where he continued to put into practice his particular methods, in such a way that in October 1918 Vatsetis, the head of the General Staff, telegraphed Trotsky in the following terms:

"Stalin's activities are ruining all my plans."

And in October 1919, Trotsky telegraphed Sverdlov telling him that Stalin's attitude meant the destruction of everything which they had been building.

Nevertheless, Stalin went about visiting all the points of conflict, applying to them more or less the same methods of repression.

In March 1919 the 8th Congress of the Party, which from then on was called Communist, took place. Proposed by Lenin with the support of Stalin, a political bureau of five members was formed, comprising Lenin and Stalin themselves, Trotsky, Kamanev and Krestinsky.

From a military point of view, the situation was improving and the Red troops under the command of General Kamenev (not the Kamenev of the political bureau) crushed the forces of General Koltchak, who had to escape to Siberia. However, in the Moscow sector the White General Denikin took Orel, at which point Stalin was sent to the sector.

In the face of this unfavourable situation, Stalin sought reinforcements; he was criticised for this by the Political Bureau, although when the Red Army cavalry was created, Stalin was finally able first to halt Denikin's advance, and finally to force him to retreat.

In spite of these victories, the civil war was not yet at an end. The White Army still occupied the whole of the Caucasus. Lenin wanted to send Stalin there, but he refused the mission, although he was later proclaimed the liberator of the Caucasus.

CHAPTER XI

THE SITUATION IN POLAND

At the beginning of March, the Polish general Pilsudski sent his troops against the Red Army, taking Kiev and occupying almost the whole of the Ukraine. The Soviet soldiers answered this attack by pushing back the Poles and finally reaching the Curzon line.

Trotsky, at that point, was opposed to continuing the advance, and Stalin showed himself in agreement. Lenin, however, took the opposite view and Stalin immediately changed his mind, positioning himself in support of Lenin and his 'speeding-up of the offensive against Poland.'

Lenin believed that a victory in Poland would make the Polish workers rise up in his support, including those in Germany.

Tukhatchevski was sent to Warsaw, without meeting any resistance and another army, led by Vorochilov and Stalin, supported the advance further to the South, trying to conquer Lvov. But Wrangel attacked in Crimea and the Central Committee sent Stalin to help Egorov and Funze, who were opposing the advance of Wrangel.

This change of posting was not to Stalin's liking, and he wrote to Lenin in the following terms:

> *I can work at the front for a maximum of fifteen days. I need a break. Find someone who can substitute me. I don't believe in the Commander in Chief's promises; he just distracts you with them...*

The Central Committee was uncertain. It sent the first cavalry division and the twelfth army as reinforcements for Tukhatchevski, so as to put more pressure on Warsaw. But Stalin again refused to obey. He wanted the troops for himself and thus be able to take Lvov. For this reason, he wrote to Kamenev:

> *The armies of the south-west front will achieve their mission, which is that of taking possession of the Lvov-Rova-Russka region, to which they are already committed. I consider that a change in the current circumstances is impractical.*

Taking advantage of this, Pilsudski launched a counter-attack which pushed back Tukhatchevski's troops over a hundred and twenty miles towards the East, with the result that in the end neither Warsaw nor Lvov were taken.

Despite this disaster, Stalin's political career was not cut short. After a short stay on the Crimean front, where Wrangel was finally defeated, he arrived in Moscow. For Stalin military operations had come to an end.

At the end of 1920, the civil war finished, but true peace did not come about until 1921. Nevertheless, the situation for the Bolsheviks was still uncertain. If they had been accepted up until that moment, it was because they represented the only defence against the previous institutions. But once the fratricidal war was over, the peasants and workers began to display their discontent against the established Soviet order.

When the 10th Party Congress began, it was said in *Pravda*:

> *The deprivations suffered by the workers are so great that their weakness has become the main problem to resolve.*

CHAPTER XII

THE POST-WAR

In 1921, the Communist Government needed to be everywhere at the same time. Russia was producing a locomotive every five days; on the other hand, during the war, the only source of energy which had been available for industry had been wood. The production of cast iron now represented 2% of what had been produced before the war. Commerce for its part had almost completely disappeared, having been replaced by barter or confiscation.

During the meeting of the 10th Party Congress, the sailors of the *Cronstadt* rose up against the dictatorship, but they were beaten and all killed on 18th March.

The new rulers realised perfectly well that they needed to alleviate the severe control which they exercised over the country. Lenin proposed to adopt a new economic policy: the NEP. This new policy served as a touchstone for the union between city and countryside. The NEP meant, according to Lenin, that they were building the economy with the peasants, whom they ought to help. On the other hand, the second aspect of the NEP was competition between state enterprises and private ones. Lenin recognised that the capitalist had supplied the country before the revolution, although, again in his own words, 'he did it badly, he did it by extortion, violation and robbery.' Now, the Soviet Government needed to show that it knew how to supply the country.

Stalin agreed with Lenin's words and shortly after said of the NEP:

> *It is a particular policy of the proletariat State, founded on the admission of capitalism, although the high commands are in the hands of socialism; based on the growth of socialist elements to the detriment of the capitalist ones; based also on the destruction of the social classes and on the construction of the bases of the socialist economy...*

The 10th Congress allowed Stalin to climb a little higher towards the summit of power. The necessity of creating a new class was recognised, since there was a need gradually to replace the tribunes, agitators and revolutionaries with inspectors, administrators and officials of every kind. In this way there would develop a new class, composed of former soldiers, former Tsarist officials and including enemies of the Revolution.

To lead this whole new machine, shrewd leaders without too many scruples were required. Some months of conspiracy, of campaigns of defamation and even of humiliation were needed to put this system into operation. Stalin was the suitable person for this work. He had on his side all the people whom Trotsky had offended in one way or another; and, in addition, he gave advice, without allowing himself to be noticed, to a number of the members who formed the Secretariat of the Party, given that whoever came to dominate this controlled the whole organisation.

In the Congress of 1921 the three secretaries who had supported Trotsky were dismissed. They were not even elected to the Central Committee. Molotov, Stalin's trusted man, was designated secretary in charge, together with Jaroslavski and Michailov, two friends of Stalin. Finally, Molotov, Mikhailov,

Stalin, when he was directing the grain deliveries from the Caucasus to Moscow.

69

Kuibychev, Ordjonikidze, Kirov and Petrovsky, all 'Stalinists', were admitted as members of the new Central Committee.

During the development of this Congress, Stalin showed himself to be extremely discreet. He only presented a report on the nationalities. The majority of the delegates did not imagine that he could come to have any fundamental role, since, in spite of being a member of numerous commissions, up until then he had not been entrusted with any important assignment.

Nevertheless, it was from the following Congress, in March to April 1922, when Stalin started to become important. At this 11th Congress, Stalin, in spite of being the head of two Commissariats, was designated for the recently created post of secretary-general of the Central Committee.

At this Congress, Preobrazhensky proposed to establish an Economburo, in the same way as the existing Politburo and Orgburo. To Lenin, this seemed a good idea, in principle – on the one hand, the Politburo, on the other, the Economburo and Orgburo. Later, however, he rejected the suggestion, arguing that he could not mechanically separate political matters from those relating to organisation, since, in addition – according to him – politics was concentrated economics.

Consequently, the Politburo centralised in itself all political, economic and organisational responsibility, and issued laws and decrees to obedient Government bureaucrats. In fact, as Lenin had said, "the communists, and he as head of them, fought against bureaucracy and fed it in front of their own noses". Lenin proposed the separation of the Party and the State, but in fact he placed all power in the hands of the party Politburo, and one day Stalin would come to turn his Politburo colleagues into mechanical puppets.

Stalin set to work. At the Congress, he did not speak on any occasion. But on its last day, the Congress had chosen a new 27-member Central Committee, which met on 3 April and chose its Politburo, enlarging it from five persons to seven: Lenin, Rykov, Kamenin, Trotsky, Stalin, Tomsky, Zinoviev, with Bukarin, Kalinin and Molotov as substitute members. At the same session, the Central Committee, in the presence of Lenin, had also chosen its Secretariat: Kuibishev and Molotov, with Stalin in the post of Secretary General. Lenin had given him his support, despite the fact that he was then in conflict with Stalin.

The Secretary General

As we have said, the Secretary General of the Party was a new post. Lenin saw it as a temporary expedient, at least while his illness lasted.

In 1922, Lenin was already a physically weakened man. The paralysis which affected him was advancing inexorably. Until 1919, there had not been a party secretary.

The 8th Congress, in March 1919, had elected Kretinsky, a supporter of Trotsky, as party secretary.

The 9th Congress had chosen a Secretariat of three: Kretinsky, Preobrazhensky and Serebryakov, all of them Trotskyites. But the 10th Congress had dismissed them and chosen three friends of Stalin. Now, in the month of April 1922, Stalin – member of the Politburo and distinguished leader – agreed to be Secretary General, and on 25th April he withdrew from his two Government posts as Commissar for Nationalities and as Commissar for Rabkrin.

Stalin understood that the Party was the central nervous system of the Soviet Union. Lenin had dominated it while he had enjoyed good health and, in consequence, the Party Secretary represented a subordinate role. But Stalin had shrewdly calculated that, with Lenin sick, the post of Secretary General could take over the party, and could even make him dictator of Russia if Lenin died.

In fact, this is what happened, and the scheme which he had plotted turned into History. Stalin ended up at the summit of Communism; he occupied it, to the exclusion of every other person, for a quarter of a century, and killed millions of human beings. The nation would discover that, as Lenin had said, Stalin was not a man of 'little intrigues'.

CHAPTER XIII

TOWARDS THE END OF LENIN

During the Congress at which Stalin was named Secretary General, Professor Felix Klemperer, a distinguished German doctor, was brought in a plane from Berlin to Moscow to examine Lenin. Also on the same mission came Doctor Otfried Foerster, an eminent neurologist, from Breslau, Germany.

It is quite possible, as we have already suggested in the previous chapter, that Lenin's state significantly influenced Stalin's final decision to abandon his two posts in the Soviet Government and take on the post of Secretary General.

Professor Klemperer, on his return to Berlin, agreed to an interview on 5th April, which was published on the following day in the *New York Times*. An extract from this interview was sent by cable to Moscow and presented to Lenin. The extract said the following:

> *Lenin is a man of robust physical constitution and great energy for work. He has worked intensely for a long time for 14 to 16 hours a day. Recently, his capacity for work has diminished, and he and his friends decided to ascertain what exactly had happened to him.*
>
> *We came almost simultaneously and we were very well received. We obtained our first information from the Commissar for Public Health, Doctor*

Semanshko, who appointed two assistants for us: Doctor Rozano and Doctor Maretzka. We examined Lenin and only found moderate neurasthenia, the result of excessive work. There were no more serious ailments, such as infection of the nervous system or the internal organism. Apart from some general prescription relating to exercise and diet, no medical prescription was necessary. We recommended Lenin to take care of himself for a period and to go for a holiday.

Those holidays were the subject of a conversation, on 6th April, between Lenin and Orjonekidze, the most preeminent communist in the Caucasus and an intimate friend of Stalin. Orjonekidze suggested that he spend a period in the Caucasus. Kamo appeared on the scene at the same time and asked Lenin to go with him to the Caucasus. Kamo was an Armenian, whose real name was Semyon A. Ter-Petrosian; he had been Stalin's comrade during their youth, in their home town of Gori, in Georgia. Before the Revolution, Stalin had used Koma to rob banks to benefit the Party treasury. It had been Kamo who, on 25th June 1907, had carried out the famous hold-up in Tiflis on the two messengers of the State Bank, and had taken possession of 340,000 gold roubles, a genuinely enormous sum of money.

Kamo had only been able to find out about Lenin's planned journey to the Caucasus from Stalin or from Orjonekidze. Lenin, without suspecting anything, had written to Orjonekidze on 9th April telling him that he had no reason to object to Kamo's company, but he wanted to know the height above sea level where the recommended house was situated, because Nadezhda Konstantinova –

his wife, Krupskaya – had heart problems and could not cope with great heights.

Stalin's idea of transferring Lenin to the Caucasus, where he would stay without communication with the Kremlin except for telegrams received from one afternoon to the next, continued on course on 17th April, the date on which Lenin again asked Orjonekidze about heights, accommodation, heating and other characteristics like that.

The Commissar for Health, Doctor Semashko, contacted Doctor Rozanov by telephone on the night of 20th April, asking him to go to visit Lenin on the following day. Professor Borchardt came from Berlin for a consultation, because it had been decided to extract the bullets which Fanya Kaplan had fired into Lenin's body in 1918. Semashko told Rozanov that Professor Klemperer had indicated that Lenin's headaches were due to poisoning produced by the lead in the bullets. However, to both doctors equally, the idea appeared quite absurd.

In the morning, Rozanov met Professor Borchardt in the hotel, and they went together, by car, to the Kremlin. In Lenin's office, and on his advice, they did without an interpreter and went to the Bolshevik leader's office. Lenin, once he was there, spoke of his headaches and of Klemperer's diagnosis. When Lenin explained that he had advised extracting the bullet, Borchardt appeared to be opposed, but moderated his disagreement so as not to undermine his colleague's authority. For his part, Rozanov explained that the bullets could not cause headaches because the organism had formed a fibrous bag around them through which nothing could penetrate. The bullet in the neck, below the right sternoclavicular, could be touched without difficulty, and he was not opposed to them extracting it. But he protested energetically against any attempt to draw out the other one from its deep bed in his left shoulder, given that it could not be reached without an extensive and painful dissection. Doctor Rozano was personally of the opinion that neither of them could cause the slightest discomfort to Lenin, and for this reason it was unnecessary to operate.

Lenin finally decided to have the operation so that the bullet in his neck could be removed; and he agreed that the operation should take place at midday on 23rd April. The operation went well. Lenin did not appear nervous and only grimaced when the extraction took place. Local anaesthetic with Novocain was used. Doctor Rozanov had announced that Lenin would leave the hospital in 30 minutes, but Professor Borchardt insisted that he remain in the hospital for 24 hours. This gave rise to the question – where to accommodate Lenin? All the rooms were full, and for reasons of security it was decide to empty a section of the women's department. Lenin himself was opposed to remaining in the hospital; but he submitted to it when he was told that he had to stay under observation.

The wound healed rapidly. In the final treatment, Rosanov asked Lenin how he was feeling and his reply was that he was not bad but that he continued, at intervals, to suffer from headaches. Rozanov recommended a vacation.

Lenin went to Gorky on holiday. There he met with two defeats. The Genoa Conference, he wrote to Stalin, was something like a real step towards a truce between the capitalist world and Russia; consequently, it was necessary to reduce the Red Army's numbers by a quarter. Lenin's proposition, dictated by telephone at half past two on the afternoon of 20th May that year, 1922, was rejected by the VTSIK four days later.

Observing the session of the VTSIK from Gorky, Lenin decided to write to Stalin proposing to him that 60% of members of the VTSIK should be workers and peasants who did not hold any post in the Soviet Government. The Politburo debated the issue on 26th May and passed the matter over to a commission.

At ten in the morning of 26th May, Doctor Rozanov received a telephone call from María, Lenin's sister. Lenin was not well: he had stomach pains and was vomiting. A car went in search of Rozanov and took him to the Kremlin, where he met with Commissar Semashko, Doctor Levin, Dmitri, Lenin's doctor brother, and various others. They all left for Gorky.

When they arrived in Gorky, a doctor who was attending the patient informed them that the vomiting had stopped, but that the headaches had not. However, there were symptoms of paresis or partial paralysis of the leg and right arm and a change in his speech.

The tests to investigate if he had syphilis were negative. Lenin's body and will struggled, clinging on to life. The patient did exercises as well as he could, rested, walked - although with difficulty - and obeyed the orders which he received from the doctors.

At the beginning of June, Professor Klemperer received a new instruction to go to Russia. When he returned to Berlin at the end of June, he explained to journalists that Lenin was not capable of carrying out cerebral work for long periods, and that he was unable to read much, because it rapidly produced headaches. He added that Lenin's illness, at those times, had nothing to do with his old bullet wounds, but rather with his last thirty years of work, which had produced an excess of tension. But he denied that Lenin was suffering from progressive paralysis.

Around the middle of July, Lenin again started to write legibly. Stalin visited Lenin. The visitor said that Lenin had told him that he was not allowed to read newspapers nor to talk about politics, with the result that, when he saw a piece of paper on the table, he moved around it in case it was a newspaper and he would break the discipline imposed by his doctors.

Stalin had been inclined to laugh at the idea, showing his short, blackened teeth. In *Pravda* he was quoted as saying:

> *I praise comrade Lenin's discipline to the skies. At the same time, the two of us joke about the doctors, who cannot understand that political professionals, received in audience, have to speak, of necessity, of politics.*

According to what Stalin said in the same edition of *Pravda*, Lenin was hungry for news and for work. He had asked about the Genoa conferences and about inflation and industry. He had been very excited to find out that the forecast for the harvests was good.

Stalin returned to visit Lenin on 15th September. In the interim, the Russian newspapers had announced a clear improvement in Lenin's health. Stalin wrote about his meeting in the special supplement of *Pravda:*

> *This time Lenin was surrounded by a mountain of books and newspapers, since he has been permitted to read and talk about politics as much as he likes. There are no traces of fatigue or excess of work to be seen. His inner calm and his confidence have returned completely. Our old Lenin, focussing his look astutely on his visitor, raising his eyes...*

In addition, Stalin explained the numerous aspects of Soviet external politics and internal issues which they had

Stalin possessed the necessary shrewdness to lead the new apparatus.

reviewed. For Lenin, according to Stalin, the worst days had passed.

But the most outstanding aspect of that supplement was the illustrations chosen by the masses. The cover showed a single photograph: Lenin, with a semi-military jacket and flat cap, and Krupskaya, with a white dress. Lenin's face and forehead appeared to have shrunk; he was trying to smile. Krupskaya appeared sad. Nevertheless, the graphic supplement did more than show Lenin alive and in a good state of health. It announced his return to work.

Lenin prepared his return to Moscow for that same month of September 1922.

A breach opened up between Lenin and Stalin. The controversy possibly took on greater bitterness when Lenin realised that Stalin wanted to seize too much power.

The problem had broken out when it was decided by Moscow to reorganise the Soviet State. Lenin, still in Gorky, mobilised his supporters against Stalin and returned quickly to Moscow.

In December 1922, Lenin's health worsened again. Since his return from convalescence in Gorky on 2nd October, his old habits of leading different teams at the same time and simultaneously urging on others, had been renewed. This was a consequence of his excitability, but it caused him to become more excitable. From 2nd October until 16th December Lenin wrote 224 letters and memorandums, held 125 meetings with 171 people and presided over 32 sessions of the Politburo, the Sovnarkom, the STO and various commissions. But on around 7th December, Lenin decided to return to Gorky, proposing to work there. But on 12th December he again returned to the Kremlin, since he wanted to talk with his deputies.

The following day he suffered two cerebral thromboses.

80

12th December 1922 was the last day on which he worked in his office. Lenin agreed to his doctor's request that he withdraw from active leadership of State affairs and went to Gorky for a prolonged break. With all this, he did not let go of the helm. He still wanted to mould decisions over important problems, such as, for example, the role of the nationalities in the planned Soviet Union.

CHAPTER XIV

LENIN'S POLITICAL TESTAMENT

On 16th December, Lenin prepared to move to Gorky. He gave instructions about what was to be done with his books and wrote a letter to the members of the Central Committee.

The doctors were insisting that Lenin go to Gorky. But snow blocked the road and no cars could make the journey. The family declared itself against the use of a sledge because of the danger and fatigue it would involve.

Stalin watched, suspiciously. He had come to the conclusion, and with good reason, that Lenin and Trotsky were forming a united front to force him to submit, or even worse, to throw him out. For Djerzhinsky knew how Lenin had reacted to his 'autonomisation' project; and besides, there was the letter of 16th December to the Central Committee: "I've now reached an agreement with Trotsky on my views with regard to the external trade monopoly..." contrary to Stalin's own opinion. Indeed, the plenary session had defeated Stalin and had accepted Lenin's proposal exactly as it had been presented and defended by Trotsky.

Lenin experienced a sensation of triumph. On 21st December he dictated a letter to Trotsky, which Krupskaya wrote in her own hand. No one knows how, but this letter ended up in Stalin's hands. We can reach this conclusion as the following day, 22nd December, Stalin counter-attacked by rebuking Krupskaya. He telephoned to inquire about Lenin's health, but took the opportunity to reprimand her for bothering her husband, providing information for him about matters which ought to have been resolved in the Party; he rained curses on her and threatened amongst other things to take her to trial in front of the Central Control Commission, the disciplinary body of the party.

It is not in fact known if she told her husband of Stalin's reprimanding phone call.

That same night, Lenin's right arm and leg became paralysed. The doctors arrived a little after dawn. On that occasion, Lenin asked for their permission to dictate every day for four-minute periods. They gave their permission.

From 23rd December, Lenin started to dictate his famous last will and testament.

The general impression we can deduce from the testament is the request that they remove Stalin from the post of General Secretary of the Party, because he had accumulated too much power. The truth is he was this and much more. Nevertheless, the question remains: given that Lenin had written in his testament on 4th January that the comrades should remove Stalin from the post of general secretary of the Communist Party, why did they not do so? He still had the political influence and the intellectual strength to be able to do so. Did Lenin believe that he would recover sufficiently to be able to attend the next party congress in March or April of 1923 and put himself at the front of the comrades that would throw Stalin out? In fact, writing a testament does not necessarily mean that one is convinced that one only has little time left to live. Or perhaps Lenin underestimated Stalin's abilities for great intrigues, while overestimating the prevailing democracy in the party that he created? Without Lenin, the party found itself powerless within the iron grasp of Stalin.

CHAPTER XV

LENIN'S END

In March 1923, after having finished his political testament, Lenin suffered a third attack on the 9th, which was the equivalent of a final sentence.

The brain of the political order had ceased to exist.

This third attack alarmed those few who knew about him. Doctor Rozanov went to visit his patient on the 11th, and noted that he had a high fever, paralysis of the right arm and leg, aphasia and fading consciousness.

A special edition of *Pravda* informed the people on 12th March of Lenin's grave illness. The Government began to publish daily bulletins. Specialists arrived from abroad. The official bulletin of 22nd March announced that Lenin's illness belonged to a category in which it was possible to make a complete recovery.

On 12th May, Lenin was transferred to a rest home in Gorky.

There he improved a bit. But now nothing could stop the inexorable process which was taking place in his brain. On his death, when the autopsy was carried out, it was found that he was affected by a very severe sclerosis.

Lenin survived until January 1924. At six in the evening of 21st January, his temperature rose alarmingly, and the ill man suffered a tempestuous attack which coincided with piercing muscle spasms throughout his body, and he lost consciousness. He was never to regain it. His life came to an end at half past six.

Lenin's body was taken to Moscow on the 23rd and was displayed for four days in the Hall of Columns. Moscow was in mourning. Many millions of people elsewhere were also in mourning. Meanwhile, beneath a fence in the Red Square, near the wall of the Kremlin, a provisional mausoleum was constructed of wood. Lenin was placed within it on the 27th. But later he was taken to a laboratory where he was mummified, and in this way his brain could be studied to find out the real causes of his death.

On 26th January, the Congress of the Soviets gave Petrograd the name of Leningrad.

CHAPTER XVI

INTERNAL STRUGGLES IN THE PARTY

After Lenin's death, Stalin confronted a conflict which he had to try to overcome: Lenin's testament would be read at the 18th Party Congress. The Secretary General knew perfectly the missing man's thoughts about his character. With the agreement of his assistants Zinoviev and Kamenev, he preferred that the testament should remain secret for ever.

In fact, this was impossible. But as soon as the first session of the Congress began, Zinoviev took the floor at the outset to say that no one doubted that Lenin's last will would have the force of law over those present; but he praised Stalin in such a way that he expected Trotsky to get up and protest. But he did not say a single word.

Zinoviev proposed that they should vote by a show of hands. The majority showed itself in favour of the continuation of Stalin as Secretary General. Next, against the wishes of Krupskaya, it was decided that the testament would not be the subject of any discussion before the party and that only the delegates could examine it. Stalin rapidly took the document and locked it up in the strongbox of his office in the Kremlin.

At that moment, serious economic problems preoccupied the Soviet leaders. The agricultural situation was not encouraging, and that same year an insurrection broke out in Georgia, under the leadership of a Menshevik-Nationalist Committee.

In the cities, the situation was fairly similar to that in the country. Industrial production had not recovered to the level before the civil war, and their buying power was far from satisfying the workers. Salaries grew more quickly than production, and for this reason it was necessary to increase this.

But the situation in the countryside was what concerned the Central Committee more. It was considered absolutely necessary to separate the 'kulaks' – rich peasants – from the poor peasants. Then it was decided to associate the poor peasants more fully with the State administration.

So, from autumn 1925, more than 10,000 communists were scattered through the farming regions to teach the less favoured the ways of cooperation.

In that year, 1924, Stalin was 45 years old and lived surrounded by a certain mystery, which reinforced his attitude still more at public meetings. It appeared as if Stalin lacked any personality. He spent hours listening to conversations without entering into the discussion and only breaking his silence to ask a question related to the issue. He did not give his opinion, but waited for an opportune moment.

To Stalin's friends, Trotsky was the true enemy. At that time he was Commissar for War and he enjoyed too much popularity for Stalin to attack him directly. He left it to two of his friends, Zinoviev and Kamenev, to look after the matter.

Trotsky would have been able to distinguish the Party and the men who led it. But he did not want to run the risk of beginning an open fight with the men who supported Stalin, since it could weaken the party and, what was almost worse, prejudice the cause for which he had dedicated his whole life. He was absolutely not prepared to do that. He therefore preferred to see his responsibilities gradually withdrawn from him, without putting up a fight other than through the medium of his writings, until, seventeen years later,

Stalin decided to dispense with the figure of Trotsky completely.

But this moment had still not arrived when, at the beginning of 1925, the two friends of Stalin, Zinoviev and Kamenev, called for the head of Leon Trotsky. But Stalin was still not in favour of repressive measures and felt that he should end with Trotskyism without eliminating Trotsky.

In the first place, he made him give up his post of Commissar for War.

When Zinoviev and Kamenev, completely dedicated in their fight against Trotsky, realised that they had left the field completely free for Stalin, it was already too late. The Secretary General of the party now took too many decisions without consulting them.

After having pitted Zinoviev and Kamenev against Trotsky, Stalin pitted Bujarin, Rykov and Tomsky against his old allies. Tomsky led the unions, while Rykov was president of the Council of People's Commissars. Each of them was an administrator as much as the other. Zinoviev, the absolute leader in Leningrad, and Kamenev, the party's administrator in Moscow, then tried to make a common front against Trotsky. But they were unable to achieve anything. When the 14th Party Congress met, at the end of 1926, Stalin was now very well-established in the party with more than 700,000 men in his support; its principal levels were also controlled by his own supporters. He counted on the support of the Red Army, thanks to the naming of Vorochilov as the new Commissar for War. And he could count on the men of the secret police.

In this and the following chapter, we will be offering a condensed biography of some of the personalities of the drama:

Grigori Zinoviev. Born in Elisavetgrad (now Kirovograd) in 1883 in the heart of a bourgeois Jewish family, in 1901 he joined the Russian Social Democratic Workers Party formed by Plekhanov, and in the following year emigrated to avoid being arrested. On the splitting of the Party in 1903 into Mensheviks and Bolsheviks – the first more moderate, the second more radical - he joined the Bolsheviks. He participated in the 1905 Revolution, and turned into one of the main leaders of San Petersburg. Arrested in 1908 and freed, he returned (as always) to Switzerland and took part in the management of various Bolshevik newspapers. Whe war was declared in 1914, he was in Galitzia with Lenin, and the two of them went to Switzerland and represented the Party at various conferences. He returned to Russia in 1917 and accepted Lenin's *April Thesis*, but with Kamenev opposed the plan for armed insurrection, although he took part in it. He was elected president of the Soviet of Petrograd. He was president of the executive committee of Communist International (1919-26). In 1924, with Kamenev and Stalin, he formed the 'troika' against Trotsky, to put himself later in the opposition against Stalin. He was excluded from the Political Bureau and expelled from the Party along with Trotsky (1927); he was readmitted, but in 1934 was condemned for ten years for involvement in the assassination of Kirov; and with Kamenev, was finally condemned to death in the first Moscow trial. In 1988, his memory was rehabilitated.

Lev Borisovich Rosenfeld, better known as *Kamenev*, was born in Moscow in 1833. Also from a Jewish family, Kamenev too became an active member of the Social Democrat Party from 1901. Imprisoned various times in Geneva, he entered into contact with Lenin and with Zinoviev. Returning to Russia in 1913, he directed *Pravda*

In Gorky, next to Lenin, when the latter started to feel ill towards the end of 1922.

and the group of Bolshevik deputies in the Duma. Exiled to Siberia in 1914, he was freed at the outbreak of the Revolution in 1917.

With Stalin he led the Party's organisation until the arrival of Lenin, with whom he was immediately in confrontation, offering his resignation as a member of the Bolshevik Party Central Committee.

After the October Revolution, he occupied posts of responsibility in the State and in the Party. Together with Stalin and Zinoviev he formed the troika, who took over power while Lenin was ill. Later he joined with Trotsky and Zinoviev against Stalin. He was expelled from the Party in 1932 and in 1938 was condemned to death, like Zinoviev.

Kliment Efremovich Vorochilov. Born in the Ukraine in 1881. A metal worker, he entered the Bolshevik Party in 1903 and in 1917 was president of the Petrograd Defence Committee. In 1918 he led the defence of Tsaritsin with Stalin. He fought against Denikin at the head of the Red Guard, and took part in the Polish-Soviet War. People's Commissar for the Army and the Navy (1925-1940) he was marshal (1935) and commander of the Northern Front against the Germans (1941); he led the defence of Leningrad. Vice-president of the Council of Ministers of the USSR (1947-53), on Stalin's death he was president of the *Presidium of the Supreme Soviet* (1953-1960), until replaced by Brezhnev. Expelled from the Central Committee (1961) for participating in the activities of the 'anti-party group', he belonged to the CPSU (Communist Party of the Soviet Union) until his death in Moscow in 1969.

CHAPTER XVII

THE FOURTEENTH PARTY CONGRESS

At the beginning of the 14th Congress, the two men who fought against Stalin, Zinoviev and Kamenev, now considered the battle lost. Stalin attacked them, fighting with the same weapons which he had previously used against Trotsky.

An unequal struggle was established: some, supporters of Zinoviev and Kamenev, sought the dismissal of Stalin. Others, the majority, silenced their voices, since they were supporters of the Secretary General.

At this time, something could still have been done to change things, but no one chose to do this.

Pravda, in an article talking about the Congress, did not mention any of the interventions of the outcasts; it simply praised Stalin's interventions and those of his supporters. There was now hardly any opposition, since it had been silenced. To end Zinoviev's influence, Stalin expelled him from Leningrad once the Congress was ended and replaced him with Sergei Kirov. He also relegated Kamenev to the level of assistant to the Politburo. And he brought about the admission to the Politburo of new members who were allied to him. Trotsky and Zinoviev remained as full members, but they were now no more than mere objects of decoration. In this way, Stalin assured himself the complicity of a broad majority of the Politburo.

Changes in agriculture

Despite this struggle for power, we should not overlook the growing economic difficulties which confronted the Soviet Government in that period.

After almost ten years had elapsed since the Revolution, the Soviet peasants were not living in better conditions than during the Tsarist era. Nor had the workers improved their situation. Salaries were very low, hunger knew no frontiers and basic commodities were in short supply.

In December 1927, at the 15th Congress, Stalin spoke about the necessity to move from small-scale agricultural exploitation to large, centralised exploitations.

This would involve the establishment of *sovjos,* or State exploitations, and *koljos,* collective farm exploitations. But to provide the necessary machinery they would, at the same time, have to speed up the industrialisation of the country.

Industry

Stalin employed a strong hand to industrialise the country. He mobilized an army of some millions of men, who were placed under the orders of engineers and technicians. These men constructed the factories, the bridges, the road and the channels. The *kulaks*, accused by Stalin of seeking to disrupt the Soviet political economy, were expelled from their lands and homes and driven into forced labour with great brutality. Those who refused were sent to Siberia, where they ended up dying.

Nonetheless, the result of all this policy of duress was that Soviet industry developed. At the end of 1928, it still did not reach a third of that of France, for example, but it had now clearly surpassed that of Tsarist Russia, even despite the First World War and the Revolution, with all the consequences which it had caused. And the most important thing is that it had been achieved without any external assistance, now that the foreign Banks refused them credit and the capitalist countries did not carry out any exchange with the Soviet Union since the new regime was in power.

Industry had grown, this could not be doubted, but not all the men in the Politburo were in agreement with the methods employed.

Bujarin was one of the men who was in disagreement, and he spoke to Kamenev, albeit in secret, about the organisations and men of the opposition.

To try to save himself, Kamenev ensured that the report reached Stalin. But he had no luck. Stalin was aware of his conversations, although to begin with it appeared that he paid no attention to the report. In reality, he was so sure of his capabilities that he did not fear them. But in contrast, he was still not satisfied with having relegated Trotsky to almost nothing, since he had played an important role during the Revolution. To free himself from this man absolutely, he proposed his expulsion from Russia to the Politburo, on 18th January 1929. The only man who dared to protest was Bujarin. But as a consequence, Rykom was dismissed from his duties as Prime Minister, a post in which he had succeeded Lenin. Tomsky, for his part, was made to relinquish the leadership of Communist International. The only person who was left alone, for the time being, was Bujarin.

Stalin had eliminated his rivals almost totally. He could finally govern almost entirely on his own. There then began the twenty-four years of Stalin's dictatorship.

Nikolai Ivanovich Bujarin. Born in Moscow in 1888. Served from a very young age in social democracy and in 1906 joined the Bolsheviks. Deported to Odessa, escaped to Germany and then set himself up in New York. On his return to Russia in 1917, he joined the Central Committee.

An outstanding technician and economist, he was one of the leaders of the communists on the Left, whose journal, *Kommunist*, he edited. The civil war and the New Economic Policy (NEP) modified his position and he ended up getting closer to the right of the party. Convinced of the remoteness of world revolution, he supported the Stalinist thesis of socialism in a single country. Between 1919 and 1929 he was a member of the Politburo and the director of *Pravda*.

After the elimination of Trotsky, Kamenev and Zinoviev, he succeeded to the leadership of the secretariat of the Communist International. Opposed to collectivisation, he joined with Rikov and Tomsky against Stalin. This time, nevertheless, he lost the game and, although partially rehabilitated in 1932, he ended by being executed in the course of one of the Stalinist purges.

Alexei Ivanovich Rikov. Born in Saratov in 1881. Affiliated to social democracy, he took part in the revolutionary movements of the beginning of the century. He was arrested a number of times and repeatedly had to take refuge in Eastern Europe. He came into contact with Lenin in Geneva (1903), aligned himself with the Bolshevik wing although in the rightist group. After the revolutionary triumph of 1917 he appeared a supporter of a government with the participation of all the socialist tendencies. In 1924 he succeeded Lenin as president of the Council of People's Commissars. Opposed to land collectivisation, he was dismissed in 1930; accused of deviationism, he was sentenced in the third of the Moscow trials, condemned to death and executed (1938). In 1988, he was rehabilitated.

Lev Davidovich Bronstein, 'Trotsky'. Born in the Ukraine in 1879. Son of Jewish peasants. Studied Law in Odessa.

Integrated himself in revolutionary circles, he started up the Union of Workers of the South of Russia in 1897. Exiled to Siberia three years later, he succeeded in escaping abroad shortly after. In London he collaborated with Lenin in the translation of *Iskra* ('The Spark') in 1902. Returning to Russia in 1905, he played a fundamental role in the Revolution as the leader of the Soviet of St. Petersburg. Deported again to Siberia, he escaped during the journey.

At the Congress of London (1907) he confronted Lenin's thesis and for some time appeared to be allied to the Mensheviks and then to Zimmervald's internationalists. In March 1917 he returned to Russia and joined the Bolshevik Party. He showed outstanding conduct in the October coup, and was made Commissar for External Affairs and for War (1917-25), a post from which he organised the Red Army and defeated the counter-revolutionaries.

Regarded as Lenin's successor, he allowed Stalin to gain the upper hand. Accused of opposition to the regime, he was expelled from the party and confined in Central Asia (1928). He abandoned the USSR in 1929 and ended up establishing himself in Mexico, where he created the Fourth International and, as we will see, was assassinated there by an agent of Stalin.

CHAPTER XVIII

CHANGES IN RUSSIA

Stalin began to govern like a true dictator at the beginning of 1929. Up until then he had been playing his game, but in a way which was to some extent hidden. In 1929, there was now no one and nothing for him to fear. He had subjugated a good proportion of his enemies, while knowing how to win himself many supporters.

That was the year of changes. From that time on, at the economic level, great progress was beginning to be seen in the Union of Soviet Socialist Republics.

Stalin was clear about the paths along which economic improvement had to start: collectivisation of agriculture and mass industrialisation. He expressed his ideas at the beginning of the year: abolition of private property in the countryside; and therefore, the most favoured rural class, the *kulaks*, had to be eliminated completely. These rich peasants amounted to 5% of the rural population. Just as he had already started to do with them before, he gave orders that, should they offer even the slightest resistance, they should be exterminated or at least exiled to carry out other types of work.

Naturally, the rich peasants did not take Stalin's decisions well, and in the countryside a real civil war broke out. The poor peasants, thinking that with the new measures their situation was going to improve significantly, supported Stalin's collectivisation. Nevertheless, owing to the prolonged resistance of the *kulaks*, collectivisation was delayed for several years and for a long time a large amount of land remained unexploited.

In addition, there was a huge task to be done: the wooden ploughs needed to be replaced by tractors; it was therefore necessary to teach the peasants how to manage these machines. And the peasants of Russia were not few: they numbered millions. And there were only instructors in the factories, so that it was necessary to start from scratch in the countryside as a whole.

To convince the Russian people of the great necessity for what he was proposing to them, Stalin harangued them with speeches in which he spoke of socialism, although he spoke also of nationalism; in this way, he half-convinced these people that they only had their native land, since Russia had become completely isolated from the outside world.

The dictator was ready to make use of everything to achieve his ends – including the sacrifice of millions of human beings. To reach his objectives, at the beginning of 1929 he established five-year plans. Little by little he came to realise that these plans were completely unachievable, especially in relation to the rural economy. Nonetheless, he did not hold back industrial growth and he sought to achieve his objectives through the means of a system of terror, employing massive deportations and, in the end, turning human beings into simple pack animals, docile beings without ideas of their own who merely had to keep in mind the words of propaganda which were pushed out according to the dictator's criterion. For his system of terror, Stalin relied on the police which he himself had set up: the GPU, which kept watch incessantly and tirelessly. At that time, to denounce an 'ignoble citizen' became a question of honour among the citizens of the vast land which comprised Russia. The concentration camps were opened and prisoners filled them until not a soul could fit in.

Besides this, that year Stalin launched a new slogan: 'In the Soviet Union there should not be more than one religion:

100

Socialism.' He accused the bishops of having incited the *kulaks* to rebel against his measures, and closed the churches and deported the majority of priests.

In truth, during the middle of the 1930s, Stalin realized that the plans which he had drawn up had not turned out as he had hoped. The rebellion in the countryside continued, meaning that collectivisation took place with great slowness, and industry did not produce the desired results. The production of iron, for example, which Stalin had said should increase more than 50% in relation to the previous year, did not rise more than 10% in 1930.

But he was not willing to acknowledge that he was mistaken. The fault for this failure was owing to the fact, according to him, that socialist-Leninist thought had not soaked deep into the souls of the citizens of the vast State. Capitalist thought still dominated. For Stalin it was, then, the moment for a new broom, to continue changing the face of Russia. To erase old ways of thinking and introduce the new Leninist-Stalinist bases.

The 16th Party Congress developed as a very well structured and faultless spectacle. It was not possible now to talk of an opposition. The speakers had learnt the lesson very well, and everything was praise for the system. In realty, fear and cowardice had taken possession of the Party's men, who saw how the dictator had quietly swept aside from the face of the Earth those who had, in one way or another, done the opposite.

Of the Stalin-Trotsky controversy, we select two documentary fragments:

Article by J. Stalin in the newspaper *Bolshevik*, 1924:

> *Does Trotsky understand the role of the party and the importance of its unity for the realisation of the proletariat? On this issue, the acts of comrade Trotsky provide the best answer. Year after year, he systematically*

101

undermines the party, weakening this vertebral column of the dictatorship of the proletariat...Clothed with the toga of the democrat in the heart of the party, following the struggles of the Mensheviks in his fights against centralism and Bolshevik monolithism. With brilliant words which say nothing, he fights against Lenin's disciples, those he confronted for 14 years, before joining our party. Appealing to young people, he is trying to oust the old guard...In the end, he thinks that it is possible to tolerate factions within the party and he himself, through his behaviour, assists in the development of differing currents at the moment of discussion.

Trotsky attacks the ideological and institutional foundations of the party. We will not allow semi-Menshevik tendencies which destroy the unity of our party, which was founded by Lenin on the basis of Leninism.

Speech by L. Trotsky in 1927:

The immediate task which Stalin has proposed is to divide the party, suppress the opposition, accustom the party to the method of physical destruction...

Stalinism finds its most frantic expression in this act. I return to repeating that these fascist methods are nothing other than the blind and thoughtless execution of the plans of other social classes. The objective which he pursues is to suppress the opposition and to destroy it physically. Now there are voices prepared to shout: "Expel a thousand and shoot a thousand others!" In this way our platform will succeed in opening up a path. The workers everywhere will ask themselves: "What is the reason why on the tenth anniversary of the October Revolution, they expel and imprison the militants of the Revolution?"

*Stalin used all propagandistic resources in relation to his personality,
as this photomontage shows.*

As can be seen, Trotsky was concerned and he was prepared for any eventuality, without suspecting that in the long term the thundering vengeance of the Red Tsar would fall on his head wherever he was.

CHAPTER XIX

WHAT WAS THE DICTATOR REALLY LIKE?

Stalin reached the age of 50 on 21st December in that year of terror. His best birthday present was the one he gave himself: absolute power.

That day, the newspapers celebrated the event with large headlines. Stalin wanted to be seen elevated like a god; he therefore had an official bust made which was supposed to be placed in all the Party cells, and an immense portrait of the dictator adorned the streets of Moscow.

Stalin had reached just where he wanted to: absolute power. Now there was no other god than him. However, the man himself lived in a simple way.

He lived in the Kremlin, but not in one of the sumptuous rooms, but in a servants' quarter, without any type of luxury. His office was furnished in a simple manner: a table, a cupboard and a small red sofa.

His character was extremely sober. Those who dealt with him said that when they were in front of him, their feelings became extremely heated. He was excessively hard with others, but he was also just as hard on himself. He was convinced of the correctness of his theories and did not allow contradiction or objections. To oppose him was to be a traitor to the Party, and the punishment in consequence can be imagined.

He did not trust anyone. In fact, he was completely alone. For him, his assistants were no more than simple puppets at his service. While they served him faithfully, they could rest easy. But if they dared to raise their voice against him, it would have been better for them not to have been born. This, in broad terms, was the character of the dictator once he had gained power.

Glimmerings of prosperity

At the beginning of 1930, things began to improve in Russia. Salaries were still very low and hunger devastated the countryside and the cities. But from 1930 onwards, some achievements would gradually come to be apparent. In a little less than four years, industrial production doubled and new cities arose, creating dams and canals. The whole world undoubtedly began to be astonished to see the resurgence of this people, albeit at a cost of so many human lives.

But the era of terror had still not ended for the inhabitants of the Soviet Union.

To ensure his own success, Stalin took new measures in 1931.

In the first place, he established what could be called a type of personal passport for the interior of the country. No one could be absent from their home for more than 24 hours without a special visa from the GPU.

In addition to this, a citizen who was declared guilty of indiscipline could be punished with ten years in prison, and even with the death penalty if he was considered a re-offender.

In the face of this situation, some opposition appeared. One could almost say that a real political rebellion broke out. All Stalin's enemies put their differences on one side and tried to unite to oppose him in a common front. Even some Stalinists tried to get the Central Committee to initiate a motion of censure against Stalin, to force him to resign. Stalin was well aware of all this, so some of those men who tried to rein in the dictator were accused as traitors and imprisoned.

Stalin knew that he had created a climate of discontent around him. He was omnipotent, but during that period he sank into a type of depressive state. He worked incessantly, and his character showed itself to be extremely irascible. To make matters even worse, his wife died at that time.

A wife's awakening

Stalin had been very much in love with his wife and until a short time before was a very happy man. But more recently, some differences had arisen at the centre of his marriage, and neither partner was particularly happy. Stalin, although in love with his wife, had never given up other women. Nadejda could not bear this, particularly when she realised that the dictator felt progressively less affection for his family. It is even said that Stalin brought a woman to his own apartment and made his wife witness his amorous scenes with his lover.

Nadejda, who was 21 years younger than Stalin, decided to start working, possibly in order to forget her troubles. Stalin agreed to this, although he did not like the idea much.

Stalin's wife was a simple person, who gained the confidence of her fellow students at the Technical School, and she therefore quickly found out about the way in which her husband governed. Nadejda was naturally horrified to find out about all the purges which were taking place at her husband's orders, even though, to begin with, she thought that he was unaware of all these atrocities.

She wanted to take an interest in all this, and her husband took measures against the people who studied with her. He ordered the arrest of everyone who had studied at his wife's side and had opened her eyes to him.

On 8th November 1932, the fifteenth anniversary of the Revolution took place and Vorochilov held a gala dinner. At this party there was talk of politics and Nadejda said nothing. Finally, she was unable to stand it any longer and exploded: she launched into a speech which was more than Stalin's ears could bear. He became more furious than anyone had ever seen him. Shouting and punching the table, he called on his wife to be quiet. But she carried on talking until all the bitterness in her heart had been emptied. Then, without exchanging a single word with those present, she withdrew to her room. The following day, the maids found her dead on her bed with a revolver at her side.

It has been impossible to confirm the truth of Nadejda's death. Did she commit suicide? Was she murdered by her husband? It has been impossible to confirm either of the two theories.

What is certain is that Stalin, from the point of his wife's death, felt himself doubly overwhelmed. He became even more isolated, abandoning his apartment in the Kremlin to install himself in Kuntsevo, near Moscow.

A step away from resignation

At this period, Stalin was uncertain of everything. His wife's death – although it would be better to say his wife's harangue in front of the Party's dignitaries – had made him doubt.

He showed this during a session of the Politburo.

Without further ado, he suggested to the members of the Council that possibly he should present his resignation for the good of the Party.

It was the moment to put an end to that man. Stalin was voluntarily offering to leave power. But no one dared to support his resignation. Everyone was fearful.

Finally, Molotov spoke, supporting him and confirming him as the sole leader of the Soviet Union. With a single phrase, Molotov confirmed Stalin at the head of power. "Continue, Stalin, continue. You have the confidence of us all, and certainly of the Party." Molotov, with this phrase, also assured his own future. For others, the opposition had just let the opportunity to finish with Stalin and Stalinism escape.

CHAPTER XX

THE ERA OF THE GREAT TRIALS

In 1933, Stalin took stock for the first time, before the Central Committee, of the Plan which had been put into action four years previously.

The statistics which he gave in that stocktaking were quite a bit better than the real ones. It is certain that the people who were in charge of statistical data exaggerated the figures so that the dictator did not become angry. Nevertheless, the basis of the speech was not totally false, since an iron and steel industry had been created which did not exist before and the production of electricity had increased considerably.

But at what cost? In fact, at a cost of the sacrifice of workers and peasants. Their salaries were very low and their labour was abundant. For this reason, a positive result was inevitable. And despite all this, they had still not reached the levels foreseen by Stalin. He therefore proposed a second Plan, which would take effect from 1933 until 1937. This second Plan was much more realistic than the first, and a little more beneficial to the workers, since animals would be handed over to the peasantry for the rearing of livestock and some taxes would be reduced in various ways.

The purges continue

Stalin still confronted an opposition. This was in reality not very effective, but it continued to exist. Stalin continued to fear Trotsky, who was the only person who did not capitulate and, in spite of his distance, continued to be very popular among the people. He had managed to maintain numerous contacts, and fought with the only means at his disposal: writing. From the outset of his exile, Trotsky began to edit a newspaper: *The Bulletin of the Opposition*, where he dared to criticise the politics followed by Stalin. This newspaper circulated in a clandestine manner, although it only reached a very small part of the population, since the great majority were illiterate and therefore only a few people could read it.

Stalin was completely convinced that many of the men who surrounded him were in contact with Leon Trotsky, since he appeared to be very well informed in his exile. Through the services of his secret agents, Stalin managed to find out that one of the leaders of the political police was in contact with Trotsky: this man, Blumkim, therefore had to disappear. He ordered him to be executed as a lesson for others. In addition, Stalin came to find out that one of those who signed the articles appearing in Trotsky's *Bulletin* was none other than Smirnov, an exile who had been pardoned a short time before and whom he quickly eliminated without further ado.

During the following year, 1934, Stalin started a contradictory political approach, based, on the one hand, on hard repression and, on the other, on measures which were to some extent liberal, granting pardons to those who renounced their past.

He abolished the GPU, which was replaced by a Commissariat for Internal Affairs; he also restricted the actions of the political police and authorised the opposition to speak in public and to write articles in the newspapers expressing their ideas. But, at the same time, he continued with the systematic and subterranean purge, with the sole aim of making the opposition disappear.

The death of Sergei Kirov

At the beginning of December 1934, Sergei Kirov, the man responsible for the Party in Leningrad, was shot dead by a young Communist. The youth, called Nicholaiev, did not offer any resistance at his arrest.

Sergei M. Kirov had been, next to Stalin, one of the most important personalities in the Politburo. He had been Zinoviev's successor, and one of the main architects of the most terrifying purges. He himself knew that by acting in this way he had gained many enemies, above all among the young.

The most widespread theory for what had impelled the young man to assassinate the leader Kirov is that Nicholaiev, who was a member of the Komsomol – that is, the Young Communists – had acted on his own account, simply to denounce, with this spectacular gesture, the growing displeasure of the young, disillusioned at the sight of the older generation giving in to dictator's ideas. Other theories were also bandied about, among them that Stalin himself had ordered Kirov's assassination because of his popularity, seeing him almost as a rival. And another possibility considered was that the order for the assassination came from the opposition, headed by Zinoviev, Bujarin and Trotsky. This was in fact the idea that Stalin caused to prevail, and it was the main accusation in the era of the great trials.

Whatever the cause, when Stalin found out about the assassination he went quickly to Leningrad to interrogate the youth personally.

And, from then on, Stalin adopted a new strategy to reduce opposition, since he realised that there was not merely opposition among the older generations, but that there was also beginning to be very dangerous opposition among the young. Therefore in future he did not order the 'misguided' to be locked up in prison or exiled to Siberia; his orders were to kill traitors.

In 1935, Russia entered a bloody period. People were completely terrified and even afraid of their own neighbours. There was no security in the Soviet Union. At any moment, one could be seized and convicted as a terrorist or a traitor – which were the same thing – and be executed without more ado.

This was what happened with Nicholaiev and those who had helped him in the assassination of Kirov. They were convicted behind closed doors and executed the following day. In fact, according to Stalin, terrorists had no right to defend themselves. Only one type of punishment was possible for this type of person: immediate death. Finally, many people were executed without even a trial being held.

It was the way of punishing the most influential opposition. The next to fall were Zinoviev and Kamenev. Stalin ordered the head of the NKVD – the old GPU – to find 'evidence' which would allow him to accuse the two men of a criminal plot and of espionage on behalf of a foreign power.

The trial

During the time that the trial proceedings lasted, Zinoviev and Kamenev were kept in a situation of semi-freedom. They were interrogated throughout the whole day, while during the night they were allowed to return to their homes. But, in spite of these efforts, the head of the NKVD was not able to obtain a confession or – what was worse – any evidence of anything which the two had done, directly or indirectly, which related to Kirov's assassination. Nevertheless

114

Going for a walk through Red Square with his immediate subordinates.

115

the two accused came to admit – and it is reasonable to assume that such a confession came under torture – that the young Nicholaiev might have been influenced by the criticism which they had previously voiced against Stalin and by the ideas expressed by the opposition in their subversive pamphlets.

To begin with, these two men were found guilty and Zinoviev was sentenced to 10 years' hard labour and Kamenev to five. But, in actual fact, this punishment was too harsh if the men were really innocent and too light, however, if they were guilty. Stalin was therefore not satisfied with the sentence. He then changed the charges and accused the two men of being enemies of socialism. At the outset, Zinoviev and Kamenev rejected this accusation. But under interrogation, Lejov, head of the NKVD, finally managed to get Zinoviev to admit that the former activity of the old opposition encouraged the degeneracy of criminals. At that point Stalin had got enough, since he knew that he could use it on the first occasion that presented itself.

Meanwhile, Stalin named Andrei Ydanov as Kirov's substitute in Leningrad. This man, if possible even more ruthless than his predecessor, employed an extremely repressive policy against the communist youth, exiling and shooting thousands of young people. Trains, by their hundreds, set out on the long journey to Siberia.

In May 1935, the Central Committee took a series of measures which decided the deaths of thousands and thousands of Soviet citizens; among these were the creation of a defence commission to put Russia in a condition to resist a possible war. Another of the measures, the most cruel possible, was to create a security commission, charged with 'eliminating' the enemies of socialism; its first task was to verify the good will and servility of Party members.

116

This security commission was composed of Stalin, Ydanov, Jejov, Malenkov, Vychinsky and Chiriatov. The first thing which this commission needed to do was to identify anyone who appeared to them guilty or suspected of an anti-Soviet attitude. Evidence was not necessary; suspicion was enough. In this way, old, new, future, certain and probable enemies of the regime came to be pilloried again.

Given that the suspects were counted in their thousands, and there were not sufficient lawyers in the whole of the Soviet Union to deal with all the trials, Stalin decided on the creation of subsidiary committees which were formed in each autonomous region to try the alleged guilty, even without them being present at their trials.

The results of these trials can be imagined: thousands of deportations, thousands of executions and thousands of disappearances without trace. In addition, as he reiterated the need for any citizen to denounce their neighbour if they considered that they were not a good socialist, the number of acts of revenge which took place through the simple method of denunciation can be imagined.

In 1936, on 14th August, the whole world found out that some of the former leaders of the Revolution, Lenin's comrades, were to be tried on the accusation of spying, treachery and terrorism. The first to be accused were 16 men, among whom were Zinoviev and Kamenev. The most remarkable aspect of the trial was that the two men declared themselves guilty and asked for the maximum penalty, without the possibility of leniency or pardon. And, naturally, after some days of trial, Zinoviev, Kamenev and the others were executed. The trial had lasted five days.

The second of these great trials was the so-called *Trial of the Seventeen*. It began on 23rd January 1937 and was a direct consequence of the previous one.

Seventeen men were accused of high treason and espionage. The accusation contended that these men were the alleged continuers of the treacheries of Zinoviev, Kanoviev, Smirnov and others and had conspired to kill Stalin. Also among the accused were followers of Lenin. One of the accused was Piatakov, a member of the Central Committee since 1921. Another of the accused was Radek, a comrade of Lenin, Zinoviev and Trotsky right from the beginning and a member of the Central Committee and the Presidium.

The trial was similar to the previous one. But only thirteen of the accused were condemned to death. The remaining four were given punishments of solitary confinement for 8 to 10 years.

The third of the great trials put in the dock Tukhachevski, marshal of the Red Army, named by Radek in the previous trial. The truth of the Tukhachevski issue would have to be sought in Germany. Hitler was preparing for war and knew that he could not confront the Soviet Army; he therefore ordered false documents to be created in order to destabilise Stalin's Army. And so not only that marshal fell, but also a large part of the General Staff of the Red Army was purged. In less than six months, three marshals, 27 generals and 20,000 officials were demoted, exiled or executed.

The fourth of the great trials was the most important in terms of the number of people placed in the dock. In total, there were twenty-one. It was also the last of the great trials, since among those twenty-one men were all those who, in one way or another, could attack Stalin. All except his worst enemy: Trotsky.

Bujarin was, possibly, the most distinguished of these twenty-one men who were put on trial. With him were also Rykov and Yagoda. All were convicted of espionage on behalf of countries hostile to the Soviet Union – Germany, Japan, Great Britain and Poland.

This fourth trial ended on 21st March 1938. Eighteen of the accused were condemned to death.

Naturally, the trials continued for some time. But the day arrived when Stalin realised that war was soon going to reach the Soviet Union.

It was then, with the forces of the opposition now greatly diminished, that Stalin decided to end the black era of Russia. He wanted, from then on, to maintain unity within the Soviet Union, in order to form a common front for the war.

CHAPTER XXI

THE SECOND WORLD WAR

Until the end of the thirties Stalin had absolutely no fears of the growing power of Hitler in Germany. For Stalin, the true enemies were the Western powers, Great Britain and France. Stalin's single compulsion, in that period, was the protection of the Soviet frontiers. For this reason, he had re-established diplomatic relations with Czechoslovakia, Bulgaria and Rumania, and had extended the non-aggression pact with Poland.

In 1935 he embarked on a new tactic and joined the Society of Nations. The USSR was seeking a rapprochement with the West.

Nonetheless, Hitler was taking up positions along the German frontier, ready to invade Europe.

Stalin had signed a pact with France in which a common front was envisaged if Czechoslovakia was attacked. But, for its part, France as well as Great Britain had signed a peace agreement with Hitler in Munich, which represented nothing less than the dismembering of Czechoslovakia. This is exactly what happened on 30th September 1938.

Having been left on his own by the Western powers, Stalin therefore decided that the only way to avoid war was to try to reach an understanding with Hitler.

121

Hitler invades Czechoslovakia

At the end of 1939, the Fuhrer demanded a colonial empire for Germany and guaranteed his complete support for Mussolini, who was claiming Tunisia, Corsica and Nice for himself.

A little later, on 14th March, when Hacha, President of the Czech Republic, who had succeeded Eduardo Benes, found himself forced to place the destiny of the Czech people in the hands of Hitler, even the most stubborn pacifists were able to realise that the curtain had just risen on the final act.

On 16th March, the Wehrmacht – the German army – started its march towards the East and quickly entered Prague. Hitler established the protectorate of Bohemia and Moravia within the framework of the Reich and offered his protection to an independent Slovakia led by a collaborator, Bishop Tiso.

On 15th April, the Foreign Office began negotiations to secure the support of the Soviet Union against Germany. But they met with a surprise.

The German- Soviet pact

In the spring of 1939, the world was moving inexorably towards war. In August, Moscow received the Reich's Foreign Minster, Von Ribbentrop, who had gone to sign a non-aggression pact valid for 10 years with Molotov, under the eyes of Stalin.

Everything had been decided on the afternoon of 19 August. Stalin had met with the members of the Politburo and had announced to them his intention to reach an understanding with Hitler. During the afternoon and night of 23rd to 24th August, Stalin, Molotov and Ribbentrop discussed the clauses of the pact. Russia claimed from Germany what it had sought from the Western powers: assurance in respect of the Baltic

States. After talking to Hitler, Ribbentrop agreed to the request. But Hitler's prompt agreement appeared suspicious to Stalin.

Stalin wanted to keep the Soviet Union out of the war. He achieved this with the pact, but it would only be for a short time.

The new Constitution

In spite of the tension which he observed across Europe, Stalin found time to enact a new Constitution, drawn up by Vychinski and Stalin himself.

This Constitution appeared to be liberal, after all the suffering of the Soviets during the period of terror. Now there was to be no fear of arrest without a court order; the Constitution spoke of respect for the home and even of being able to choose a defender where necessary.

But the application of this new Constitution would not be so much to the Soviets' liking. The head of the NKVD, Lejov, took good care to ensure that arrests were legal. On the other had, with the imminence of war, Stalin officially abolished some of the rights which were established by the Constitution. So, for example, the right to work was replaced by two decrees according to which a worker could only leave his job with legal authorisation. And when war broke out, Stalin disregarded every one of the articles of the Constitution.

The assassination of Leon Trotsky

Furthermore, after the purges of the previous period, only those loyal to Stalin remained in the USSR. The new generations had been brought up to adore the idol.

There only existed one person who continued to trouble Stalin and that person was no other than Trotsky himself. Now finally exiled in Mexico, Stalin decided to finish off his bitterest enemy once and for all. On 20th August 1940, the Catalan Ramón Mercader assassinated Trotsky at his home near Mexico City, despite the fact that he was very well protected. Stalin now had nothing to fear from Leon Trotsky. And the death of the old Soviet leader did not cause much international disturbance, at least during those moments of tension in Europe.

Ramón Mercader had managed to gain the confidence of the internationalist leader and his family, to the point of becoming the Russian politician's secretary. To carry out the crime, Mercader made use of an ice axe or mountain climber's pick, which had a sharp iron point.

It was not the first time that Trotsky was the object of an attempt against his life. Already on another occasion there had been an unsuccessful attempt to assassinate him by machine-gunning his house. Mexico was the last stage of an exile which had began in January 1928 after his deportation to Alma-Ata in Central Asia, along with his principal followers. This was when his doctrine of permanent and universal revolution got its name, being called *Trotskyism*.

Exiled from the USSR, he sought asylum in Turkey, where he continued writing his autobiography and the history of the Soviet revolution, naturally from his own point of view, although that does not prevent both works being two important – if subjective – sources for the understanding of the period and to compare judgements.

From Turkey he went to France in 1933 and to Norway in 1935, from where he was expelled under pressure from the Soviet Government. Hitler's victory in Germany dissuaded him from his plan to reform the Communist International, and he therefore began the formation of a loyal Fourth International, while he encouraged his supporters in the creation of their own parties, based on his revolutionary perspective.

With his daughter Svetlana, one of the fruits of his marriage to Nadejda.

From the first moment of his exile, Trotsky did not stop denouncing Stalin's regime as a bureaucratic and Bonapartist perversion of the dictatorship of the proletariat. According to his theory of permanent revolution, Stalin's regime, isolated from world revolution, was condemned to disaster.

CHAPTER XXII

THE ADVANCE OF THE WEHRMACHT IN EUROPE

The crisis in Europe was becoming more imminent by the hour. On 1st September, in the morning, German troops entered Poland. A tremendous force was bringing England to its feet, already immersed in an irreversible process. On 3rd September, at nine in the morning, the ambassador of Great Britain handed Ribbentrop an ultimatum warning Germany to withdraw its troops from Poland.

But this ultimatum only allowed three hours, and it was therefore somewhat absurd to think that it could be accepted by Hitler. So from that morning the whole of Europe was on the brink of war.

The German-Soviet pact had been accepted by the Soviet people as something necessary to avoid war.

But the rapid advance of the German Army into Poland left Stalin astonished. The pact foresaw that the Red Army should immediately penetrate Eastern Poland. From 5th September, Von Ribbentrop pressed Moscow to meet its commitments. Meanwhile, Stalin put him off, since he was not very certain that the Western powers would not accuse him of participating in the division and of following the Nazi dictator's game. Then again, he was also not very certain that the Russian officers would not turn against the German soldiers.

Nonetheless, on 17th September, the Red Army crossed over the Soviet-Polish border. The Germans were now near, and therefore the intervention was merely a protective measure.

In a few hours the Soviets were able to occupy the eastern part of Poland. The following day, the German and Soviet armies met. Poland had been swept from the map.

The invasion of the countries of the North

Von Ribbentrop appeared in Moscow to divide up the Polish territories and to organise the ones that lay between the two countries. Germany reserved for itself the whole of ethnic Poland. The Soviet Union persuaded the three Baltic states, Latvia, Estonia and Lithuania, to sign a treaty of assistance and to cede some air and naval bases. Some months later, the Governments of these three countries would be overthrown and the countries themselves annexed by Moscow, and turned into federal republics. Before returning to Berlin, Von Ribbentrop visited Stalin to invite him to a meeting with Hitler in Berlin. Stalin at first declined the invitation. But on the day of his 60th birthday he sent a telegram to Hitler:

> *The friendship of the peoples of Germany and the Soviet Union, strengthened by blood, has every reason to be long-lasting.*

He also took advantage of the moment to sign new pacts with Berlin. In a secret protocol, Germany and the USSR undertook to suppress all propaganda which advocated the restoration of Poland, and they sought immediate peace in a common declaration, blaming England and France for the continuation of hostilities. From then on also, the commercial agreement began to bear fruit, since Germany received raw materials and wheat from the Soviet Union, while the latter received machinery and equipment.

Stalin then fixed his attention on Finland and decided to invade it, in spite of the protests of Sweden, Norway and Denmark, expressed through the US President Roosevelt. But Stalin did give way. His sole idea was to fabricate an incident between Finland and the USSR. He therefore announced on 23rd November that the Finnish artillery had opened fire across the frontier and that as a result of this action five Soviet soldiers had died; he therefore denounced the non-aggression pact signed in 1932 and ordered the bombing of various Finnish cities, Helsinki among them.

The war between the USSR and Finland lasted four months. At the beginning, the small Finnish Army stood up to the Red Army, which was ill-prepared to fight against the harshness of a cold 20 or 30 degrees below zero. But the Soviet Army finally got the upper hand through its strength of numbers. Hostilities ended in the middle of March 1940. Finland had to abandon Viborg and the isthmus of Careia. The USSR had won this war, but had come out of it badly. The prestige of the Red Army had now declined substantially.

The hero of the defence of Finland against the Russians was the marshal *Baron Carl Gustaf Emil Mannerheim*. He was born in Villnas, near Turku, in 1867. He served in the imperial Russian Army from 1887 to 1917 and took part in the Russo-Japanese war with the rank of lieutenant general, and in the First World War led an army corps. After the 1917 Revolution, he returned to Finland where he was entrusted with the command of the Finnish liberation troops. Chosen as regent of the new Finnish state, he obtained recognition from their allies of the independence of Finland in December 1918. He withdrew from politics when Stahlberg was raised to the presidency, and from 1931 to 1939 was head of the

Council of Territorial Defence. After leading the country' resistance against the Soviet invasion in 1939-40, he was promoted to marshal in 1941.

With the intention of recovering the lands lost in 1940, he began the fight again alongside Germany, when Germany invaded the USSR. From July to August 1941, the Finnish forces reconquered the land lost to the North-East of Lake Ladoga and in the isthmus of Carelia they took Viborg and established themselves in the Soviet fortifications beyond the frontiers in 1939. From September, the army of Carelia penetrated into Soviet territory between the Onega and Ladoga lakes and cut the Murmansk-Leningrad railway line.

From 1942 to 1944, calm reigned along the whole front, but on 9th June 1944 four Soviet armies began a violent offensive against the Isthmus of Karelia and Soviet Karelia, until Finland was forced to retreat back to the frontiers imposed in 1940. Although Viborg fell, it was possible to hold the front. Soviet Karelia was evacuated. Mannerheim, chosen as president of the Finnish republic, began negotiations with the USSR. The armistice signed in Moscow specified the severing of relations with the Third Reich. Then the Finnish troops turned against the German mountain troops installed in the North, which withdrew towards Norway. Mannerheim, declared a 'national hero and saviour of the country', abandoned his political functions in 1946, dying in Lausanne in 1951.

The fight for Finland between Swedes and Russians goes back to the 12th and 13th centuries. Although Sweden won the battle for centuries, from 1721, during the reign of Tsar Peter I the Great, fortune turned in favour of Russia, which began to occupy the Finnish territories, until Tsar Alexander I of Russia took the title of Grand Duke of Finland after a new war in 1809. In 1917, with the Tsar overthrown, Finland proclaimed its independence, which was recognised by the

Bolshevik Government in 1918. In 1919 the Republic of Finland was proclaimed. In the period between the wars from 1918 to 1938, a period of political stability and economic recovery began, which was shattered again in 1939.

CHAPTER XXIII

HITLER INVADES RUSSIA

At the end of spring 1940, Hitler ended the invasion of France. Pétain signed the armistice with Hitler, on 22nd June. England, for its part, found itself under the threat of the German bombers commanded by Goering.

This Franco-British disaster left the way free for Hitler. And it was then that the Fuhrer started to cast his eyes on the territories of the Soviet Union.

The Red Army had been severely depleted, in the first place because of the purges which it had suffered under Stalin's yoke, and in the second because of the harsh conditions encountered in Finland.

Stalin knew that if Hitler wanted to attack him this was the moment to do it, and that he would not fail to take advantage of the situation when he had mustered sufficient forces on the eastern front. The armament industry in the USSR there-fore worked day and night.

On 19th October 1940, Von Ribbentrop wrote to Stalin offering him a pact between Germany, the Soviet Union, Italy and Japan to take possession of Europe and the rest of Asia.

On 12th November, Molotov travelled to Berlin, with orders from Stalin to appear friendly, while at the same time not agreeing in any way to the Fuhrer's demands over the Baltic countries. Hitler, through Ribbentrop, repeated his offer to Stalin of a pact between the four countries already mentioned, to assure himself of the total defeat of Great Britain. In return for the pact, he offered India to the Soviet Union, while Italy and Germany would appropriate the African possessions for themselves, and Japan those of South-East Asia.

Molotov put the matter off. On his return to Moscow, and after some days of reflection, Stalin replied expressing his conclusions: to sign the pact, he would require the immediate withdrawal of the German troops in Finland and the recognition of Bulgaria as within Russian influence.

Hitler could not accept these conditions without definitely forsaking an attack on the USSR. He therefore refused Stalin's conditions out of hand. Stalin had succeeded in gaining some months, although perhaps not all the time which he needed to reorganise the Red Army.

From then on, Hitler prepared to invade the Soviet Union.

In April, Stalin signed a reciprocal neutrality agreement with the Japanese Minister for Foreign Affairs. He would therefore not have to fight on two fronts.

Stalin knew that Hitler would not delay an attack. He was well aware of his plans. What he did in fact not know was when the attack would begin.

The attack finally began on 22nd June 1941. That day, at dawn, the German armies crossed the Soviet frontier to strike towards the East along a 1000-mile front. Operation Barbarossa, the name given by Hitler to the attack on Russia, had begun.

There was no surprise in the rest of Europe. Churchill, for example, had been expecting it for some time. Nobody had really believed in the German-Soviet pact of 1939. From then on, Great Britain would not be facing the German enemy alone.

On that day, 22nd June, 166 Axis divisions rushed towards the Russian steppes from the Barents Sea to the Black Sea. 4,600,000 men were launched in the most daring action conceivable: the destruction of the USSR and its communist regime.

A terrible period began both for the Soviets and the Germans.

In Moscow the news of the invasion began to arrive, but nobody really wanted to believe it. Stalin preferred to believe that it was simply a German provocation and not a proper invasion.

But the news which was coming in was too clear for it not to be believed. On top of this, the German ambassador in Russia asked to be received to deliver an urgent message: "Germany had declared war." The news dropped like a bombshell in the Politburo.

The first measures to be taken were to mobilise all reservists born between 1905 and 1918 in a territory of 14 military regions, and to declare a state of war; this was announced the same day on all radio stations throughout the Soviet Union.

Molotov was responsible for giving the news to the people.

> *This morning, at exactly 3.45 AM, without any declaration of war and without the Soviet Union having provoked any confrontation, German troops have attacked our country and have bombed cities including Jitomar, Kiev, Sebastopol, Kaunas and other towns and villages. For the moment, more than two hundred people have been killed. It appears that there have been air raids and artillery attacks launched from Romania and Finland. This attack against our Soviet Union is an act of treachery, without precedent in the history of civilised countries. They have betrayed a pact, whose clauses we have respected at all times with the best intentions...*
>
> *This war has not been brought to us by the German people, but by its tyrants, by its governors, by the bloodthirsty German leaders, by those men who have already reduced to nothing a nation friendly to us,*

135

as was France, our dear Czechoslovakia, Poland, Serbia and other countries...In 1812, the Russian people rose up to crush Napoleon, who tried to reduce us to nothing. Today, comrades, the Government calls on you, men and women, to stand shoulder to shoulder with the glorious Bolshevik party, the actual Soviet Government and our dear leader, comrade Stalin. The cause of the Soviet people is a just cause, and for this reason the enemy will be crushed without prejudice and victory will be ours, yours, a victory of all the Russian people.

For some time, Stalin showed no signs of his existence. He gave no message to his compatriots. But on the morning of 3rd July, he decided to make a patriotic harangue:

Comrades, brothers, sisters, fighters of our army. Today, 3rd July, I address you, my friends!

A grave threat has loomed over our country. The German enemy has succeeded in taking Lithuania, some areas of the Ukraine, a section of Lithuania and the eastern part of Byelorussia. I ask you: is the enemy invincible? No. We know from experience that the armies of Napoleon and William II appeared invincible. And yet they ended up being defeated and crushed...

This war against the fascists will be yours. In the occupied territories, guerrillas must extend guerrilla warfare through all parts where the Red Army cannot reach. But if the enemy advances, it will not be able to find anything of which it can take advantage. Not a single machine, not a drop of petrol, not a single loaf of bread...all usable goods which cannot be removed should be destroyed.

His fear of the opposition led Stalin to order the death and imprisonment of traitors.

In addition, I say to you: in our country, cowards are not possible. Whoever hinders our work will be judged by military tribunals, whatever his rank or position.

But there is more. I also have to say to you that Churchill's historic declaration of British support for our dear Soviet Union, and the decision of the Government of the United States, which has decided to help us, cannot be received by our country with other than a profound feeling of gratitude. Comrades, our forces against the cruel enemy are immense! Our power must be put into movement to crush the Hun!

This speech caused the hoped-for effect in the Soviet people. Almost for the first time, the people knew that they had a leader on whom to rely.

While the fighting continued, in the Kremlin work carried on without a break. The German forces advanced towards Leningrad, Moscow and Kiev.

On the front, the first objective was to stop the advance of the German Army. In Moscow, defences against armed vehicles were built around the city. Resistance was organised in this way.

Gradually the rumour began to circulate that two German tanks had been seen in Khimki, the suburb to the north of Moscow. It was 1st October and a wave of panic took over the city. The embassies and a certain number of Government services were ordered to evacuate to Kuybichev. Two days later a state of siege was proclaimed, although two million people had already been evacuated.

The offensive against Moscow had effectively been unleashed on 30th September. On 2nd October, Hitler had announced the final assault on the capital.

On 5th October, Jukov had been called from Leningrad to organise the defence of the city with Sokolovski, Koniev and Rokossovski, the best Soviet strategists. On the 30th, a first German offensive was stopped. On 7th November, in Red Square, Stalin harangued the troops which were leaving to defend the city, telling them of their great ancestors. The Siberian divisions had just arrived to support the Army.

The second German attack on Moscow took place on 16th November. It was repelled 6.2 miles from the capital. In December, the Soviets decided to launch a counter-attack. The battle for Moscow was won. In the northern and southern flanks, the enemy was forced back 186 miles from Moscow. In the south-east, the forces of Von Rundstedt had to retreat. Rostov was recovered by the Red Army. During that harsh Russian winter, the cities of Leningrad, Moscow and Sebastopol contained the enemy onslaught well.

By January 1942, Moscow had been saved. But the winter campaign planned by Stalin and Chapochnikov became stuck in the snow. Stalin had just been designated Commissar for War. He therefore had all power in his hands: as secretary general of the Communist Party, president of the Defence Committee, President of the Council and of the People's Commissars. The highest authority in the country controlled all its operations.

An appointment in Moscow

In all his communications with his ally in England, Winston Churchill, Stalin asked for the opening of a second front which would alleviate the Red Army a little. Churchill, for his part, studied the possibility of a landing in North Africa. For this reason, the British Prime Minister decided to meet with Stalin in Moscow.

Churchill arrived in Moscow on 12th August 1942, one month before the appearance of the Nazi armoured divisions in the suburbs of Moscow. Stalin had already had news of the German operation through his secret services, and was completely determined not to allow the armoured divisions to cross the Volga.

The visit of Churchill – accompanied by Roosevelt's delegate Harriman – lasted five days. Churchill was very keen to get to know the dictator. Stalin represented for the Duke of Marlborough's descendant everything that he hated most: that is, Communism. In addition, he had decided to put an end to his thoughts of opening a second front in Europe, as Stalin had asked for with such insistence in all his communications.

Harriman attended the first meeting in the Kremlin. The meeting lasted a little more than four hours. That night a dinner took place at which Stalin again insisted on the issue of the second front. But Churchill would not concede. He brought Stalin up-to-date on the preparations for the Anglo-American landing in North Africa and Stalin immediately pointed out the advantages which he saw in this incursion in Africa: on the one hand, it would attack Rommel from behind; at the same time, it would succeed in intimidating Spain, arousing the French against the Germans in France itself, and finally, making Italy bear the main burden of the war in Europe. Churchill was impressed by the analysis which Stalin made. Nevertheless, he absolutely refused Stalin's repeated request, and the meetings ended in disagreement.

Then Stalin decided to put pressure on Roosevelt. Through his former ambassador in Washington, Stalin caused the rumour to circulate that the Soviet Union could be considering an agreement with Hitler. Roosevelt then quickly sent Wilkie to obtain a meeting with Stalin. Stalin urgently requested a declaration of the opening of a second front, at least to raise the morale of the Soviet people.

Meanwhile the war continued on the Russian front. The Germans advanced towards the Volga, occupying Kurban and marching towards Baku. On 18th August, the Germans had reached the right bank of the Volga, and the circle was closed around Stalingrad. On 13th September, all hell was let loose in this city; the German army was not annihilated here until 2nd February 1943. The Kremlin had become the only command headquarters.

Stalin was surrounded by strategists and coordinators. He had at his side Timochenko, Vorochilov and Vassilievski. From that moment on, Soviet morale would start to improve and, to the contrary, that of the German army would fall. Gradually they re-conquered the lost territories.

On 13th July, the German offensive was halted. 2,900 German tanks were destroyed, and around 70,000 soldiers died in the course of a gigantic battle. On 5th August, Orel and Bielgorod were recovered.

At the end of June of that year, the German offensive on Kursk was imminent. Some weeks before, the Germans had retaken the city of Kharkov. Stalin then thought about the need for a conference with his English and American allies.

There are enough reasons to state that the decisive turning-point of the Second Word War, when this change of fate took place, was chronologically in November 1942, the period when the Soviets began encircling the German Army at Stalingrad, the English crowned their victory at El Alamein and the Anglo-Americans landed in North Africa. At the same time Germans and Italians occupied Vichy France militarily, putting an end even to the fiction of a government already in absolute subordination to its overlords.

In spite of his high losses during the previous winter, Hitler wanted to unleash a new offensive with the summer of 1942 hardly started. In May the Battle of Kharkov began; in June, the Germans arrived, as we have already said, at the bend in the Volga and in June the beginning of 'Operation Stalingrad' was ordered. Also in August 1942 the Germans reached the Caucasus and crowned Mount Elbruz.

The German dictator was not unaware of the weakness of his ground troops and of the air force of the Reich, but he relied on the Russians having exhausted their last available reserves in the course of the winter. Moreover, the Fuhrer's objective was now limited: to take possession of whatever remained of supplies in Europe and in particular of the oil in the Caucasus. Hitler issued his military leaders with orders that they should not be affected by any humanitarian feelings regarding the Russian civilian population.

At the beginning of winter, the German troops of the Caucasus now had to fight in retreat, although in reasonable order. Hitler forbade the Sixth Army commanded by Von Paulus to make the slightest retreat; on reaching Stalingrad, it had encountered a bloody resistance from the population in the ruins of the city. The Fuhrer appeared to be obsessed with the desire to take the square which bore the name of his mortal enemy; he blindly launched his best shock troops against Stalingrad, but they met with a resistance which would amaze the world and would largely decide the result of the Second World War. Air raids and artillery shelling on a vast scale destroyed and devastated the city. The defenders clung on desperately to their enclosure, fighting in caves, on parapets, among the ruins, obstinately obeying Stalin's orders to fight to the last soldier, to the last bullet.

Hitler was so convinced of his victory, that he announced that he had taken the city in a communiqué, but in the middle of November General Zukov unleashed a counter-offensive with plentiful stock of excellent artillery and with well-equipped forces which were numerically superior. His men broke the German front and cut off eighteen top German divisions using a pincer movement. In the recovery of the city, 24 German generals, among them Von Paulus, and 91,000 soldiers were taken prisoner, not without heroic resistance, in which over 200,000 men fell in the fighting.

CHAPTER XXIV

THE TEHRAN CONFERENCE

During the days from 28th November to 1st December 1943, Stalin, Roosevelt and Churchill met in Tehran, the capital of Persia or Iran, to discuss three important subjects: the future Organisation which would guarantee peace, the creation of the 'second front' and the Japanese question.

It was the first time that Stalin had gone abroad, and he had prepared for it in detail, from his daughter Svetlana's report on the customs of the Americans and a description of Roosevelt's character, to security measures which included the prohibition of the installation of microphones in the rooms allocated to the American President. Beria was responsible for this kind of measure, but he asked for the employment of his agents, and they were turned into service personnel of all types with such perfection that their chief, Krulev, received the post of Minster of the Interior as a reward.

Stalin was to come face to face again with Churchill, who appeared this time in uniform and presented him with the 'Sword of Stalingrad', which the dictator kissed respectfully. He approached the meeting with the intention of breaking the Anglo-American solidarity and winning the President over to his side. During her stay in the United States as a guest of the White House, Svetlana had the duty of writing to her father weekly, telling him all the details, and through her he knew of Roosevelt's nonconformist character, his personal style of dealing with matters of state, and the overwhelming friendliness with which he disarmed his opponents.

The real problem which worried Stalin was the position of the Soviet Union in the future, since in earlier conferences the creation of an Organisation was taking shape which was not at all similar to the Society of Nations, and he was fearful of being excluded by a conspiracy of 'capitalism'. Stalin, who had dissolved the 'Komintern' and on 15th March 1944 would replace 'The International' as the State anthem, felt serious concerns about the role destined for the Soviet Union in the world order. The course of the war had created the concept of the "three great powers", referring to Great Britain, the United States and the USSR; he wanted to prolong this way of thinking. He judged that with peace, America would concentrate on its hemisphere, leaving England remaining as the only protector of Europe. Time would show him his mistake over this, caused not by the wishes of the United States but by Soviet obstinacy in relation to the occupation of Germany and Austria.

The three countries had already begun a trial in Italy, with the running of the 'Allied Consultative Council for Italy', of which the members were Vichinsky, for the USSR, MacMillan, for Great Britain, Robert Murphy, for the United States, Massigli, for France and representatives of Greece and Yugoslavia.

Stalin's idea for launching himself into classic international politics, or rather for participating in the pre-established game of the Chancelleries and moulding it to his own methods and systems, was to take advantage of the idea which they offered him with the classification of 'great' and 'small' powers. Hence one of his apparent contradictions: to deny the admission of France to the Tehran Conference on an equal footing, despite the fact that the USSR was the first Government to recognise the Committee of De Gaulle. He wanted to restrict the number of the 'great' powers at the same time as giving a permanent character to this situation.

146

The meeting of Stalin and Roosevelt was the origin and root of the 'Cold War' and of the appearance of two new concepts: those of East and West. The Georgian met a man who was open, optimistic, talkative, who showed him how to use a smile as a weapon of combat. Every night Roosevelt visited 'Uncle Joe', without any other company than a Russian interpreter. They chatted about plans for the future, criticised their collaborators and at every moment created a climate of intimacy which led Stalin to say: "one believes oneself to be in the presence of friend who one has known for many years before; his affectionate and intimate behaviour leads you to that point."

Nonetheless, once Stalin had come through his first moments of being dazzled, he took advantage of all Roosevelt's words. If for the President they were dinner-table pleasantries, for the dictator they were concessions and verbal agreements to be wielded at the opportune moment. In addition, in the face of such generosity, Stalin did not hesitate to present the Soviet Union as a poor people, which justified its revolutionary expansion, a poverty increased by the war. Roosevelt did not hesitate in assessing the Soviet Union's losses at 10,000 million dollars, an argument which Maiski would wield at the Yalta Conference, basing it on what the President had said.

Stalin found the way open to discuss as difficult an issue as that of war reparations and suggested that it should be Germany who should foot the bill; this would permit swift development of the Soviet economy. He presented a panorama of the destruction of industries, of chemical and oil installations at the hands of the Germans, for which he thought that Germany, once defeated, should pay. However, Roosevelt, who then believed that the war would not end until 1947 or 1948, with the result that Germany would by then be totally devastated, accepted that as compensation for a debt already valued he could advance in the long term the amount of 3,000 million dollars. Stalin accepted, but suggested that it should go as high as 5,000 million.

All these issues were discussed and agreed outside the framework of the Conference, and for this reason Churchill was not even made aware of all this.

Another of the subjects discussed over the dinner table was the position of the USSR in relation to Japan. In the official meetings, Stalin used the argument that he was receiving the whole brunt of the German attack and was therefore not in a position to be able to fight against the Japanese at the same time. What is more, in the face of the Wehrmacht's oppression, he asked again for the opening of a 'second front'.

In these chats outside the framework of the Conference, he reached an agreement about the recovery of the Kurile Islands and the southern half of Sakhalin and even the Manchurian Port-Arthur Darien railway. Roosevelt accepted this and proposed the signing of a document, but Stalin preferred that it should remain a verbal agreement, for fear that the Japanese would attack the Soviet Union before the defeat of the Reich. When Molotov, in 1946, reminded them of these matters, the Anglo-Americans rejected them, since not even the State Department had any knowledge of them.

Another issue dealt with in the same way was the case of Turkey. Stalin reported that the Muslim troops that fought alongside the Germans, troops conscripted in the Caucasus and Crimea, officially counted as Turks. He proposed that he should be authorised to take action in the Straits, basing his view on some reports between Von Papen and Ismet Inonu, according to which Turkey could annex the Transcausus and Batum as soon as the Germans conquered Baku. Roosevelt opposed this, and proposed a revision of the Montreux Convention; he secretly offered the USSR a base in the Eastern Mediterranean, either at the port of Cirenaica or in the Dodecanese. When Molotov

His second journey outside the USSR took place at Potsdam in July 1945.

made this public in Lancaster House in 1947, the world would be astonished.

Churchill intervened on the border problem. Stalin asked for Prussia and proposed the creation of the Independent States of Bavaria, Rhineland and Westphalia. Roosevelt wanted at all costs to apply the 'Morgenthau Plan', which meant converting Germany into an agricultural country and dismantling its industry. Churchill supported this idea, but Stalin opposed it.

Then they dealt with the opening of the 'Second Front'. Stalin relied on the considerable benefit of the victories of Stalingrad, Kursk, Orel and Dnieper, and was the first to communicate to Roosevelt and Churchill the existence of the new German armament, ranging from their efforts to make a released atomic energy bomb to the reality of the V1s and V2s, as well as new types of aeroplanes, capable of reaching a speed of 600 miles an hour.

The American Secret Service was completely unaware of this news; the Intelligence Service knew about it through having placed one of its agents in the Soviet network the Red Chapel. Highly impressed, Roosevelt did not hesitate to inform Stalin about the existence of the 'Manhattan Project', which was key to his knowledge out about the development of the atomic bomb.

Stalin sought oil concessions in Iran, at which point Churchill and Roosevelt closed their ranks. The President argued that the time for colonialism had passed and that, in any case, he had given assurances to the head of the Iraqi Government, Saltan, that new concessions would not be authorised.

The Tehran Conference emphasised three principal points for the future. According to its communiqué, the 'Second Front', the International Bank and the UNRRA were created. An agreement was reached as regards the range and timing of operations from the East, the West and the South. In this way, *Operation Overlord* got off the ground and was scheduled for the beginning of May 1944.

CHAPTER XXV

THE YALTA CONFERENCE

The war with Germany was reaching its end. The Red Army was relentlessly overrunning all of Eastern Europe. The Normandy landing had taken place and had achieved success.

Then, as he had done before, Winston Churchill wanted to go to Moscow to have a meeting with Stalin. On 9th October 1944, Churchill arrived at the Kremlin accompanied by Anthony Eden. Churchill was anxious to sort out the Balkan issues. The Russian Armies were in Romania and Bulgaria.

Churchill, seated opposite Stalin, wrote on a sheet of paper the division of territories, which was as follows: Romania, 90% for Russia and 10% for others. Greece, 90% for Great Britain and the U.S. and 10% for Russia. Yugoslavia, 50% for Russia, 50% for Great Britain and the U.S. Hungary, 50% for Russia and 50% for Great Britain and the U.S. Bulgaria, 75% for Russia and 25% for Great Britain and the US.

This was Churchill's proposition. Stalin simply limited himself to ratifying the proposition on the sheet of paper which the British Prime Minister presented.

The Conference of Yalta – or Crimea, as Stalin preferred to call it

The war reached its end, both in Europe and in the Far East. It was necessary for the three allies – Stalin, Churchill and Roosevelt – to meet urgently.

The Soviet dictator imposed his will and chose the venue for the meeting. It would be Yalta, on the banks of the Black Sea, on the Crimean peninsula, on 3rd February 1945.

In the USSR subtle changes had taken place, which world public opinion and very possibly the American Secret Service were unaware of.

Stalin had to give a daily account of what was taking place to a special committee headed by Molotov, in which the members were Beria, Malenkov, Bulganin, Vorochilov and Mikoyan, as well as another military one in which General Poskriebychev figured as representative of the Politburo, and the dictator's General Staff comprised Marshal Antoniev, the Air Marshal, Khudiskov, and Admiral Kuznetov.

Stalin established himself in the palace of Prince Yussupov, Rasputin's assassin, where he was able to rely on direct communications with the Headquarters of Zukov, Koniev and Rokossovski, the three marshals with effective command of the troops, and with those of Timochenko and Vassilevski. Twelve Soviet Army corps had been put on the march with a human potential that can only be imagined in figures: on the Bulgarian-Greek frontier there were 20 divisions, and on the Polish frontier 180 - meaning that the Balkans and the Danube valley up to Bratislava had fallen into the Russian zone of influence.

Yalta began with the spectre of Poland; Roosevelt maintained his Russophilia to the extent of prohibiting private meetings between the Secretary of State, Stettinius, and the British minister, Anthony Eden.

Roosevelt tried to sort out the Polish dispute in a private conversation, since a breach between the Soviet Union and each of its allies was taking shape. Stalin agreed to the incorporation in the Lublin Government of representatives of London, and that elections would take place in the territories of the future satellite states, in order later to prevent the entry of the Polish parties and to maintain his intransigent posture.

Another of the points of friction lay in the issue of the veto of the future Organisation of Nations, as well as the number of positions which Russia could count on. Stalin wanted the Ukraine and Byelorussia to be considered as States, which Roosevelt agreed to in face of Churchill's view.

The result of Yalta was that all the Balkans were subject to Russia influence, apart from Greece; that the USSR would count on three votes in the UN, and that Poland was sacrificed once again; that Stalin would not declare war on Japan until Germany was defeated and that the Politburo adopted a political line, inspired by Marshal Bulganin, whose principal points were those set out below:

> *The Anglo-Saxon powers have only admitted the Soviet Union into their close political circle as a last resort, when faced by the threat of the Third Reich, which wanted to replace the bourgeois Anglo-Saxon control over the world with Germanic control.*
>
> *The Soviet Union will have to adopt the following policies: 1. – Prevent the formation of a unified Germany, which could be created from the confederation of various States reunited under the power of economic necessities, unless the Soviet Union exercises an effective and permanent control over the central organs of this Germany. 2. – Set up governments controlled by the local Communist parties in all the countries of the Soviet zone; use these parties in countries outside the Soviet zone so that their representatives participate in their respective future governments, and thereby create a political influence which prevents them turning into instruments of aggression against the Soviet Union. France and Italy appear of*

153

particular interest in this respect. 3. – Not allow China to recover its unity and to encourage the Communist Government of Yen-Nan in its fight against the Government of Chun-King. See to it that communist representatives enter the latter's government with the objective of advocating a Chinese Confederation whose northern part would be under the influence of the Soviet Union.

These political rules were agreed by the Politburo a few days after the Yalta Conference.

In truth, no international conference was ever held with so much high drama. Roosevelt was dying. For his part, Churchill attended the macabre spectacle, only being able to save France in return for handing over six nations to Russia.

In Yalta it was also agreed that the future occupied Germany would be divided into four zones, against the view of Stalin, who wanted France to be left without any part. The German high command was also eliminated forever.

For the first time, Stalin explained to the other two great powers the military situation in the USSR and made them listen to a talk by Colonel General Antonov – not without having first pointing out that he was doing so as a spontaneous initiative, since he did not feel obliged to allow anyone to interfere in the Red Army's plans.

This was, in general terms, how the Yalta or Crimea Conference went.

CHAPTER XXVI

THE END OF THE WAR

On 12th January 1945, seven Soviet armies began the offensive from the Baltic to the Danube. On day 15 of the offensive, the 180 Soviet divisions were 180 miles from Berlin; on day 17, Warsaw was conquered; on day 18, they penetrated Silesia and took Kattowice, Sosnowice and Krakow; on day 23, Bromberg fell, and from there they carried out an encircling manoeuvre with Danzig at the northern extreme and Poznanin to the West, with the result that Eastern Prussia was isolated.

The Soviet Army began a large operation to isolate Pomerania, and at the beginning of February Zukov conquered Schneidemuhl, near the old German-Polish frontier of 1939. Danzig and Gdynia were taken on 30th March.

Finally on 16th April the final Soviet offensive began with Berlin as its goal. The Armies of Zukov and Koniev attacked in the direction of Wriezen and Luckenwalde; Rokossovski crossed the Oder and advanced towards Mecklemburg. The 62nd Army, which General Chuikov commanded, was the first to arrive in Berlin. This Unit was formed from the defenders of Stalingrad.

The Red Army began to bomb the Chancellery, where Hitler was in refuge, on the night of 26th April. As the concrete exploded in pieces, the whole refuge trembled. For the Germans, it was very difficult to put up even the slightest resistance. The Soviets were less than two miles away, and the proud army of the Wehrmacht was no more than a group of ragged marionettes seeking vainly to try and save their lives.

On 28th April 1945, Mussolini was captured by some Partisans when he tried to escape. He was executed and strung up by the feet, as was his lover, Clara Petacci.

Then on 28th April, Hitler became aware of the treachery – according to him – of Himmler, when he received a despatch in which Himmler was said to have got in touch with Count Bernadette, from Sweden, to discuss conditions for surrender.

On Sunday 29th April the news arrived at the German Chancellery that Mussolini had been captured and killed. It appears that Hitler decided, before this event, to put an end to his life as soon as possible and not meet the same fate as Mussolini.

That same Sunday, the Soviet Army were only two blocks from the Chancellery of the Third Reich.

Finally, on 30th April, in the depths of the bunker, Hitler ended his life at the same time as his wife Eva Braun.

Two SS men took Adolf Hitler's body from his room, covered in a blanket, and took it up to the garden. They did the same with the body of Eva Braun. Then Guensche, one of the Führer's assistants, poured petrol over the bodies and set light to them.

The end of the Third Reich

During the night of 30th April, General Krebs, who was the only one who knew how to speak Russian, went – preceded by a white flag – to meet General Chuikov, the leader of the siege of Berlin.

General Chuikov demanded from Krebs the unconditional surrender of the bunker and of the troops in the capital, and when Krebs told him of Hitler's suicide, the Soviet general replied that they had already been informed.

For his part, Doenitz, the new Führer thanks to Hitler, who had named him his successor, spoke to the German people insisting on the need to destroy the Bolsheviks, warning that if the Allies did not understand the significance of that decision, they would also be considered enemies.

Finally, and despite Doenitz, the Wehrmacht surrendered on 1st May on the Italian front. On 3rd May the English entered Hamburg. The armistice was signed in Reims, and began to take effect on 8th May at 11 a.m. exactly.

One man who had not been able to see the ending of the war in Europe had been the American President.

Franklin Delano Roosevelt, the man who had succeeded in being re-elected President of the United States four times, died on 13th April, at his country house in Warm Springs as a result of a brain haemorrhage.

Roosevelt had been born in Hyde Park, New York, in 1882. The cousin of President Theodore Roosevelt, whose niece Anna Eleanor he married in 1905. He studied at the prestigious Harvard University. In 1910 he was elected Democratic Senator for the State of New York and during Wilson's term of office he was Secretary of the Navy (1913-1921), a post from which he strengthened the American fleet; after the breach with Germany (1917), he was made responsible for the inspection of U.S. naval forces in Europe (1918). Democratic candidate for the Vice-Presidency in 1920, he was defeated and retired to his legal activities. In 1921 he became victim of polio which marked him all his life, although it did not interrupt his political career. He was Governor of New York (1929-1933). As Democratic Candidate for the Presidency of the U.S., he promised the 'New Deal', beat Hoover (1932) and took over at the moment in which the

U.S.A. was going through its worst economic crisis in its history.

In 1933 he recognised the USSR, although he maintained some reservations, but he was concerned about the totalitarian regimes of Hitler and Mussolini and tried in vain to calm their war-mongering tendencies. He had to overcome isolationist public opinion, which believed that France and England could stand up to them. He had a law passed to sell war material to the allied combatants, and once France had been defeated he lent war material to the British and Soviets. The Japanese attack on Pearl Harbour (on 7th December 1941) followed by Germany's declaration of war (11th December) increased Roosevelt's responsibilities: he had to lead the U.S. war effort, equip his allies, decide on the development of the atomic bomb and prepare for the post-war. To do this he met up several times with Churchill, and both of them met Chang Kai-Shek, the representative of the Chinese nationalist party, besides the Tehran and Yalta Conferences with Stalin already mentioned.

The Potsdam Conference

In the middle of July of that same year, 1945, Stalin travelled for the second and last time outside the USSR.

The Potsdam Conference was the longest of the three held during the War. It lasted from 16th July to 2nd August 1945. Stalin found himself facing two men whom he did not know.

It should be remembered that Churchill, who had recently resigned after the ending of the war, was not re-elected at the ballot box – this had been a heavy blow for the old lion. Attlee had been the winner in Great Britain. Roosevelt – as will be recalled – had died shortly before the end of the war. Therefore, Stalin's two counterparts were Attlee and Truman, although

The representatives of the victors of the Second World War.

Churchill participated in some sessions before knowing the results of the elections in Britain.

On the USSR side, those attending the conference were Stalin, Viacheslav Molotov, Commissar for Foreign Affairs; Nikolai Kuznetov, Commissar for the Navy; the Head of the Army General Staff, Marshal Aleksei Antonov, and the Head of the Navy General Staff, Admiral Zucherov.

For Great Britain those attending were: Winston Spencer Churchill and his Foreign Secretary, Anthony Eden, until the day when they had to give up their positions to Clement R. Attlee and Ernest Bevin, in their respective offices; Lord Leathers, Minister for War Transport, Sir Alexander Cadogan, Permanent Secretary of the Foreign Office; Sir Alan Brooke, Chief of the General Staff; Sir Andrew Cunningham, Admiral of the Fleet; Sir Hasting Ismay, Chief of the General Staff of the Ministry of Defence, and Field Marshall Sir Harold Alexander, Supreme Allied Commander in the Mediterranean.

For the United States those in attendance were President Truman, the Secretary of State, James F. Byrnes; the head of the presidential General Staff, Admiral William D. Leahy; the head of the General Staff, General Marshall, the Commander in Chief of the Fleet, Admiral Ernest J. King; the Commander in Chief of the Air Force, General Henry H. Arnold, and the Special Ambassador, Joseph E. Davies.

The Third Reich and Hitler had already ceased to exist when these men met in the former palace of the imperial crown prince. For the journey to Berlin, Stalin travelled in a train of twelve coaches, four of which were historic relics, since they belonged to the Tsar's train and Trotsky had used them for his famous propaganda tour during the civil war. A long route through Lithuania was chosen so as to avoid Warsaw.

At Potsdam, Truman tried to assume the role of Roosevelt, organising musical evenings, where he played Stalin's favourite pieces on the piano; despite this, he did not succeed in warming the atmosphere. The first friction was caused by the very rigid censorship rules imposed by the Soviet authorities on the Press correspondents, who had to confine themselves to describing the number of meals and visitors; they were not allowed to attend the sessions or to stay in Potsdam. The only thing which they knew was that Truman presided over these meetings at the request of Churchill and Stalin.

On 19th July, the English newspaper the *Yorkshire Post*, considered as Eden's mouthpiece, wrote in its editorial:

> *This rule of silence is frankly unfortunate. The closed barrier of secrecy which has been put up around this Conference annoys us, especially because what is happening during these days in Potsdam concerns each and every one of us, men, women and children.*

It was certainly impossible to know much until the publication of the final communiqué:

> *The British and United States Governments have taken measures to protect the interest of the Polish Provisional Government, as the recognized Government of the Polish State, in the property belonging to the Polish State located in their territories and under their control, whatever the form of this property may be. They have further taken measures to prevent alienation to third parties of such property. All proper facilities will be given to the Polish Provisional Government for the exercise of the ordinary legal remedies for the recovery of any property belonging to the Polish State which may have been wrongfully alienated.*

The three Powers are anxious to assist the Polish Provisional Government in facilitating the return to Poland as soon as practicable of all Poles abroad who wish to go, including members of the Polish armed forces and the merchant marine. They expect that those Poles who return home shall be accorded personal and property rights on the same basis as all Polish citizens.

The three Powers note that the Polish Provisional Government, in accordance with the decisions of the Crimea Conference, has agreed to the holding of free and unfettered elections as soon as possible on the basis of universal suffrage and secret ballot in which all democratic and anti-Nazi parties have the right to take part and to put forward candidates, and that representatives of the Allied press shall enjoy full freedom to report to the world upon developments in Poland before and during the elections.

The following agreement was reached on the western frontier of Poland. In conformity with the agreement on Poland reached at the Crimea Conference the three heads of Government have sought the opinion of the Polish Provisional Government of National Unity in regard to the accession of territory in the north and west which Poland should receive. The president of the National Council of Poland and members of the Polish Provisional Government of National Unity have been received at the Conference and have fully presented their views. The three heads of Government reaffirm their opinion that the final delimitation of the western frontier of Poland should await the peace settlement. The three heads of Government agree that, pending the final determination of Poland's western frontier, the former German territories east of a line running from the Baltic Sea immediately west of Swinemuende, and thence along the Oder River to the confluence of the western Neisse River and along the western Neisse to the Czechoslovak frontier, including that portion of East Prussia not placed under the administration of the Union of Soviet Socialist Republics in accordance with the understanding reached at this Conference and including the area of the former free city of Danzig, shall be under the administration of the Polish State and for such purposes should not be considered as part of the Soviet zone of occupation in Germany.

The Conference agreed upon the following statement of common policy for establishing, as soon as possible, the conditions of lasting peace after victory in Europe.

The three Governments consider it desirable that the present anomalous position of Italy, Bulgaria, Finland, Hungary and Rumania should be terminated by the conclusion of peace treaties. They trust that the other interested Allied Governments will share these views.

For their part, the three Governments have included the preparation of a peace treaty for Italy as the first among the immediate important tasks to be undertaken by the new Council of Foreign Ministers. Italy was the first of the Axis powers to break with Germany, to whose defeat she has made a material contribution, and has now joined with the Allies in the struggle against Japan. Italy has freed herself from the Fascist regime and is making good progress toward the re-establishment of a democratic government and institutions. The conclusion of such a peace treaty with a recognized and democratic

163

Italian Government will make it possible for the three Governments to fulfil their desire to support an application from Italy for membership of the United Nations. The three Governments have also charged the Council of Foreign Ministers with the task of preparing peace treaties for Bulgaria, Finland, Hungary and Rumania.

The conclusion of peace treaties with recognized democratic governments in these states will also enable the three Governments to support applications from them for membership of the United Nations. The three Governments agree to examine, each separately in the near future, in the light of the conditions then prevailing, the establishment of diplomatic relations with Finland, Rumania, Bulgaria and Hungary to the extent possible prior to the conclusion of peace treaties with those countries.

The three Governments have no doubt that in view of the changed conditions resulting from the termination of the war in Europe, representatives of the Allied press will enjoy full freedom to report to the world upon developments in Rumania, Bulgaria, Hungary and Finland.

As regards the admission of other States into the United Nations organization. Article 4 of the Charter of the United Nations declared that:

1. Membership in the United Nations is open to all other peace-loving States who accept the obligations contained in the present Charter and, in the judgment of the organization, are able and willing to carry out these obligations;

2. The admission of any such state to membership in the United Nations will be effected by a decision

of the General Assembly upon the recommendation of the Security Council.

The three Governments, so far as they are concerned, will support applications for membership from those States which have remained neutral during the war and which fulfil the qualifications set out above.

The three Governments will not support any application from Spain for membership of the United Nations.

The conference examined a proposal by the Soviet Government concerning trusteeship territories as defined in the decision of the Crimea Conference and in the Charter of the United Nations Organization.

After an exchange of views on this question it was decided that the disposition of any former Italian territories was one to be decided in connection with the preparation of a peace treaty for Italy and that the question of Italian territory would be considered by the September council of Ministers of Foreign Affairs.

There will be taken into account the interests and responsibilities of the three Governments which together presented the terms of armistice to the respective countries, and accepting as a basis the agreed proposals.

The conference reached the following agreement on the removal of Germans from Poland, Czechoslovakia and Hungary: The three Governments having considered the question in all its aspects, recognize that the transfer to Germany of German populations, or elements thereof, remaining in Poland, Czechoslovakia and Hungary, will have to be undertaken. They agree that any transfers that take place should be effected in an orderly and humane manner. Since the influx of a large number of Germans into Germany would increase the burden already resting on the occupying authorities, they consider that the Allied Control Council in Germany should in the first instance examine the problem with special regard to the question of the equitable distribution of these Germans among the several zones of occupation. They are accordingly instructing their respective representatives on the control council to report to their Governments as soon as possible the extent to which such persons have already entered Germany from Poland, Czechoslovakia and Hungary, and to submit an estimate of the time and rate at which further transfers could be carried out, having regard to the present situation in Germany. The Czechoslovak Government, the Polish Provisional Government and the control council in Hungary are at the same time being informed of the above and are being requested meanwhile to suspend further expulsions pending the examination by the Governments concerned of the report from their representatives on the Control Council of Germany. During the conference there were meetings between the Chiefs of Staff of the three Governments on military matters of common interest.

Approved by Joseph Stalin, Harry S. Truman and Clement R. Attlee.

CHAPTER XXVII

THE 'COLD WAR'

When the war in Europe ended, Stalin was faced with an economic situation of the greatest complexity. On the one hand, the United States appeared to be a country which had not suffered the direct consequences of the war, since its citizens remained unharmed and flourishing. The Soviet Union, however, needed to rebuild hundreds of villages and cities and to return to achieving industrial production like that before the War, at least, if not better. And there was also a need to undertake the reform of a completely devastated agriculture, continuing at the same time with ration books and reconstructing agricultural machinery.

Only Finland and Romania contributed their part by way of war reparations, while in the Kremlin they had to sign a financial agreement with the countries of Eastern Europe to cover the gigantic costs of the reconstruction of the country.

Faced with this panorama, the reconstruction of the Soviet Union began in the first place with the security of the State itself. The Soviet population needed to be convinced of the necessity of continuing to maintain Communist traditions in the USSR, since the influences which the Allied powers had been able to spread during the War were dangerous for the State. In the Press, the traditional attacks against capitalist imperialism reappeared. The censors confiscated translations of English and American authors, which were judged to be dangerous. This struggle against ideological contamination was very important. The frontiers of the USSR were quickly closed and, slowly, the wartime allies were turning into post-war enemies.

For his part, Stalin showed himself intolerant of the cities in which there had been the beginnings of collaboration with the Nazis. The traitors were shot and hundreds of people were exiled.

The war heroes, as announced immediately after it ended, were also punished. Despite the fact that the decisions were made with great care, Marshal Jukov's fall into disgrace was resounding. Some months after the victory, Jukov was summoned from Germany and received the command of the military district of Odessa; in this way he was deprived of all popularity.

The atomic bombs of Hiroshima and Nagasaki

On 8th August 1945, the Soviet newspapers spoke of the dropping of the first atomic bomb on Japan. The second bomb, on Nagasaki, was announced much later. The Soviets quickly understood the significance of these bombs and their implications. At the moment the bombs were dropped, the equilibrium between the forces in the world was broken. The bomb represented a serious threat to the USSR.

Stalin rapidly met with his experts in the Kremlin. Joseph Stalin assigned himself the presidency of the nuclear research committee. The political direction, the laboratories, the industrial factories designated for the production of the bomb, were put under Beria's control. The first atomic bomb would explode four years later in the Ust-Urt Desert, between the Caspian and the Aral.

But financial problems also increasingly confronted two of the three great powers. Truman abolished loans to the USSR, which irritated the dictator greatly. It was not only this which annoyed Stalin, but the fact that Truman tried to recover rapidly the interest on the loans which Roosevelt had granted the USSR.

In consequence, two years later, Stalin rejected out of hand the support plan named the Marshall Plan. All the countries of the East did the same.

By 1948, three years after the war ended, Stalin had managed to get those States which he had under indirect control into a situation of direct control. In every State, in one way or another, communism had triumphed, and the secret police employed under the direction of Soviet advisers had taken its place in the Party. Stalin could feel satisfied with himself.

Failure in Yugoslavia

It was from March 1948 that Stalin fine-tuned his tactic against Tito. The latter had broken finally with the King Peter and elections had been called in Yugoslavia. The Popular Front had gained victory.

Stalin reproached Tito for his independence and his refusal to provide the Soviet commercial mission, which had been installed in Belgrade, with important economic reports. Tito had also rejected the Soviet plan drawn up in 1947, which did not allow any place for heavy industry in Yugoslavia. He reproached him, moreover, for a commercial agreement with Great Britain. According to Stalin, Tito would have to give his surpluses over to the Soviet Union, and the Soviet market would have sold them for its own profit.

Stalin had carefully drawn up his plan to end disagreements with Tito. He counted on a certain number of supporters in the Central Committee of the Yugoslav Communist Party, and tried to cause a meeting of the Committee to take place, by means of a letter from the Soviet Central Committee to the Yugoslav Central Committee. Tito and his supporters, in a clear minority, would be excluded and imprisoned. But Tito had realised Stalin's trick and ordered the Stalinists to be imprisoned.

The split had just been confirmed. Stalin, seeing that he had failed, ordered Yugoslavia to be expelled from the Kominform.

Failure in Berlin

Everybody was resigned to the division of Germany. In fact, no one had expected it to last such a long time.

On 20th January 1948, Sokolovski denounced Anglo-American attempts to integrate West Germany into a Western military and political bloc.

On 10th March, after a somewhat violent debate on the prohibition of the unified socialist party in the western zones, he declared that any discussion from then on was useless.

On 31st March, Sokolovski informed the American commander Clay that, to improve the administration of the Soviet zone, some Russian officials would control in advance the baggage and identities of travellers who used the western military trains to Berlin. Clay protested, but it was no use, since the Kremlin had ordered that all trains should be stopped and searched meticulously at the boundary of the Eastern zone.

Finally, from the end of May, military traffic between Berlin and the rest of the world was practically cut off.

On 26th June, Truman decided to supply the city by air until a diplomatic solution to the issue was found.

On 3rd July, the Western commanders met with Sokolovski. He left the meeting very clear that the difficulties would continue until the United States, Great Britain and France renounced their plan to create a government of the three zones.

Stalin confronted his former allies after the Second World War.

To show that his decision was not going to be reconsidered, Truman decided, with Attlee's agreement, to send the atomic bomb to Great Britain.

On 2nd August, Stalin received three diplomats in Moscow: Smith, on behalf of the U.S.; Chataigneau, on behalf of France; and Roberts, on behalf of Great Britain. Stalin had understood that he could now go no further. He appeared very friendly and explained that he had absolutely no intention of forcing the Western powers to leave Berlin. And he proposed the introduction of the Eastern Mark in the Soviet zone, in East Berlin, as the same time as the lifting of the transport restrictions and the withdrawal of the Western Mark.

But Sokolovski was unaware of the agreement in principle which had been concluded in Moscow. Or, at least, he acted as if he was unaware of it. Nonetheless, the airlift had made Stalin's strategy fail and the blockade ended in 1949.

CHAPTER XXVIII

THE END OF STALIN

In the middle of October 1952, the 19th Congress of the Soviet Communist Party took place, the first to be held since the war had ended.

Stalin spoke the closing words, and consequently received the applause of those present. But he had not given the report on the activities of the Party. This time it had been Molotov who had had responsibility for doing this. Stalin, by that time now old, was suffering from arteriosclerosis and had a weak heart.

At that time the Soviet Union had already achieved the "A" Bomb and was on the point of achieving the "H" bomb. Stalin was content. He had managed to restore the balance with the West.

In the USSR, Stalin's word was sacred. Thanks to Communist propaganda, the fearsome dictator had turned into a demigod. Beria, at his side, played a decisive role in the USSR.

But Stalin was not now the man he had been before. He had grown old and lived in an almost unreal world, dominated by his own fantasies. His apartments in the Kremlin were full of policemen, as was his farm. Svetlana, his daughter, was not able to see him and had to communicate with him through Beria.

Convinced that his personal effort was indispensable to take his plans forward, he wanted to prolong his life as it was.

He made famous a book by Bogomoletz, one of his doctors, *"How to prolong life"*, in which he explains numerous treatments, blood transfusions after cancer operations and the application of an anti-conjunctival serum of his own invention.

At the beginning of winter 1952, Stalin suffered a new attack. The diagnosis of the doctors who were summoned did not leave any room for doubt: arteriosclerosis. Stalin needed to get right away from political circles and rest, far from the capital. But Stalin did not want to rest. More than that: he accused the doctors who signed the diagnosis of having tried to get rid of him, with the result that, through Beria's intervention, the professors were accused of having worked for the international nationalist bourgeois organisation, a Zionist espionage organisation which worked for the American secret services. They were also accused of having poisoned Ydanov and Tcherbakov, and of having tried to assassinate the marshals Gorovov, Vassilievsky and other military figures by means of poison. Two of the doctors died under torture.

But, in any case, this whole charade would not succeed in prolonging the life of the god Joseph Stalin. Various theories about his death were bandied about: Did he die from poison? Was he struck down by a heart attack or an embolism? Did he die in Moscow or did he die on his farm at Kuntsevo?

The only certain facts are provided by the various testimonies of people who saw him alive a little before the news of his death was given. So, among others we have the Indian ambassador Menen, who would say:

> *Stalin appeared absent throughout the meeting. During my visit, he did nothing more than spend all the time filling whole sheets of white paper with images of menacing wolves, which he drew with a blue pencil.*

Another of the testimonies was Khrushchev's:

It was a Saturday afternoon when Stalin invited us to dinner at his country house. He appeared in good form and it turned out to be a very agreeable evening. Afterwards, we all returned to our houses. Stalin had the habit of telephoning every one of us on Sunday, to discuss unresolved matters. But that Sunday he did not call, and it seemed strange to us all. Then, the head of the guard called us to tell us that he was ill. Beria, Molotov, Bulgarin and I myself went quickly to Kunntsevo to see him. He was already unconscious. He had suffered a brain haemorrhage which had paralysed an arm, a leg and his tongue. We were at his side for three days but he did not manage to recover consciousness. Then, for an instant, he seemed to come out of his coma and we all returned to his side, while a nurse fed him with spoonfuls of tea. Stalin took us by the arm and tried to joke with us, smiling weakly.

Another testimony, that of Ilya Ehrenburg, indicates:

At six in the morning of 6th March 1953, Soviets who had put on their radio sets found out the news that Stalin had died. The Russian people became completely afraid. They found out, through the news bulletins, that the master of the Soviet Union had breathed his last breath the day before, at ten minutes to ten.

For eight hours, taking advantage of the night, the secret police had surrounded Moscow. At five past nine, on 5th March, the medical report even spoke of collapse, arrhythmia and leukocytes. But it was now a long time since the Russian people had forgotten that Stalin was a man of flesh and blood.

There are few genuinely reliable facts. To all appearances, however, Stalin's illness did not begin with the brain haemorrhage on the night of 2nd March. In fact, it was preceded by multiple pathological symptoms of a psychophysical character which lasted some years.

It appears that from 2nd March, after Joseph Stalin's cerebral haemorrhage, the Soviet leaders held a long conference meeting in the Kremlin; this would contradict the statements of Krushchev, who said that everything happened at Kuntsevo.

Stalin was embalmed like Lenin and was buried right next to his predecessor.

Demythification

It was in fact Khrushchev himself, then in power, who in 1956 would take responsibility for demythifying the god Stalin.

The closing session of the 20th Communist Party Congress had finished, and the Soviet leader had called together the main leaders of the USSR to attend an extraordinary prepared session in the Kremlin.

Khrushchev had to read a secret report, in which it was said that Lenin's ideological successor had not been worthy of this title. At the beginning, there was timid applause among those present. Then, frenzied applause. That night, in the Kremlin, the ghost of Stalin was buried.

CHRONOLOGY

1879 — Joseph Vissarionovitch Djugachvili is born on 21st December in a humble house in the city of Gori.

1888 — Joseph Vissarionovitch Djugachvili enters the religious institution of Gori.
— Joseph's father, aware of his son's entry into the theological school, takes him to work with him in the Tiflis shoe factory. His mother nonetheless manages to get Joseph to enter the institution again.

1890 — Joseph's father, Vissarion Ivanovitch, dies.

1893 — Joseph graduates from Gori School and enrols at the Tiflis Theological Seminary.

1895 — Nicholas II, the new Tsar of Russia, continues the implacable policies of his predecessor's autocratic regime.

1896 — In August, Joseph, who is now calling himself Koba, joins the Third Group, a movement of revolutionary intellectuals.

1898 — The Marxists of Tiflis take charge of the newspaper *Kvali*. Joseph – Koba – Djugachvili has turned into a true socialist.

— Trotsky is arrested after two years of activities as a social democrat revolutionary. He is exiled to Siberia.

1899 — Koba decides to leave the Tiflis seminary and returns to Gori.

— Lenin publishes his first book, *Development of Capitalism in Russia*. Fights against economism and populism, with other orthodox Marxists, led by Plekhanov.

— In December, Joseph Vissarionovitch finds a job as assistant in the Geophysics Observatory in Tiflis. He had earlier been a tutor to an Armenian in Gori but he grew bored.

1900 — Appearance of the newspaper *Iskra* (The Spark), edited by Lenin. Examples of the subversive newspaper are introduced in Russia.

1901 — The police search Stalin's room in the Observatory. In consequence, Stalin loses his job and has to act clandestinely, hiding himself in Tiflis.

— On 5th May, Stalin takes part in a street demonstration, where he makes his first speech in such a large gathering. The demonstration is dissolved in a bloody manner and with many arrests. Stalin escapes to Gori.

1901 — In November, Stalin is one of the 21 delegates at the conference in Tiflis of the Social Democrats group, which takes place in Avlabar. The Conference organises a new Social Democrat committee for Tiflis, of which Stalin is a member.

— In December, Stalin goes to Batum.

1902 — In January Stalin and Kandelyaki organise the Social Democratic Committee of Batum; it organises a clandestine publication in Stalin's house.

— Stalin is arrested for the first time on 18th April and remains in the prisons of Batum and Kutais until the end of 1903.

1903 — In February, Stalin is elected a member of the Caucasian Federal Committee in his absence, on the occasion of the first congress of the Social Democrats of the Caucasus.

— On 25th July, Stalin is condemned to three years' exile in Siberia.

— The second congress of the Russian Social Democrat Workers party takes place (in Brussels and London), ending with the split into two factions of Bolsheviks and Mensheviks; a Central Committee of three Bolsheviks is elected. Trotsky will join the Mensheviks, although for a short time.

— In winter, Lenin leaves *Iskra* on its 51st edition.

1904 — Stalin arrives at Novaya Uda, to begin his three years' exile.

— On 9th February, the Russo-Japanese war begins.

1904 — Stalin returns to Batum, having fled – it is not exactly known when.

— Possibly in November, Stalin joins the Bolsheviks.

— Trotsky breaks with the Mensheviks and remains outside both factions until 1917.

— Stalin marries Catalina Svanidze in Tiflis.

1905 — This is the year of the first Russian Revolution.

— On 9th January the events of what has come to be called Bloody Sunday take place.

— The Strikers' movements spread through all parts of Russia.

— The Third Congress of the Social Democrat Workers' Party, in which the first congress of the Bolsheviks take place.

— Stalin's first leaflet appears.

— On 27th June, the uprising on the warship *Potemkin* takes place.

— In July, a Soviet is organised in Kostroma. The mutineers of the Potemkin are handed over to the Romanians on Constanza.

— Peace between Russia and Japan is signed on 5th September at Portsmouth, New Hampshire, through the intervention of President Theodore Roosevelt.

— At the initiative of the All-Russia Railwaymen's Union, a political strike led by the Mensheviks begins across the whole country.

— This succeeds on 20th October.

— On 21st October a general strike begins, led by the Bolsheviks.

— On 9th December, Trotsky is elected president of the Soviet of St. Petersburg. On 16th, the Tsarist

Presiding over a demonstration to celebrate his 70th birthday.

Government arrests the whole of the Soviet of St Petersburg.

1905 — That month Stalin attends a conference in Tammefors, Finland. There he meets Lenin.
— In the same year, Stalin's son, Yasha, is born.

1906 — In the month of April Stalin is arrested and freed during the course of a search of the printworks at Avlabar.

1907 — Stalin's wife dies in April.
— Stalin attends the 5th Congress of the Social Democratic Workers Party in London. There he hears Trotsky speak for the first time.
— Lenin establishes himself in Kuokalla, Finland, while Stalin returns to Tiflis, to organise the raid on the Public Treasury.
— In July, Stalin takes up residence in Baku.

1908 — In April Stalin is arrested and held in prison. In September he is exiled to Siberia.

1909 — Stalin escapes from his exile in Siberia and returns to Baku.

1910 — Stalin is arrested again and is exiled to Siberia, where he will remain until 1911.

1911 — In February Stalin writes a letter to Lenin.
— In July, with his sentence completed, he returns to St Petersburg under the alias of Chizhikov.
— Stalin is arrested again in St. Petersburg and exiled to Vologda, this time for three years.

1912 — Stalin escapes from Vologda, going first to Baku and then to St. Petersburg, where he presents himself to the Russian Bureau of the Central Committee.
— Stalin is arrested on the same day on which the first edition of *Pravda* comes out.
— Stalin begins his fifth exile, in Narym.
— Stalin escapes from Siberian exile for the fourth time and arrives in St. Petersburg in September with the pseudonym of Vassyliev. He travels to Krakow and then returns to St. Petersburg.

1913 — Stalin attends the Conference in February in Krakow. He passes by Vienna and has a chance meeting with Trotsky.
— Stalin is arrested for the last time shortly after his return to St. Petersburg and is exiled to the Arctic Polar Circle.

1914 — The First World War breaks out in Europe.

1917 — This will be the year of the February and October Revolutions.
— In February the first demonstrations begin and the strike widens to result in a general strike.
— The exiles in Siberia are freed.

- Lenin arrives at Petrograd (the former St. Petersburg).
- On 1st May this day is celebrated as a festival freely for the first time in Russia.
- In July Stalin succeeds Zinoviev as informant at the Bolshevik Conference in Petrograd.
- In September, Stalin meets his future wife, Nadejda Alliluyeya.
- The October Revolution begins. Lenin leaves his hiding place and appears at the meeting of the Petrograd Soviet. Operations take place against the Winter Palace, seat of the Provisional Government.
- On 15th November, Stalin and Lenin sign the Declaration of Rights of the Toilers and Exploited Peoples.
- On 8th November the Winter Palace falls and the Provisional Government is arrested.
- On 9th November the first Council of the People's Commissars is organised: Lenin is elected President of the Council; Trotsky is put in charge of foreign negotiations; Stalin is named Minister for Nationalities.

1918 — On 3rd March the armistice is signed in Brest-Litovsk.
- The Soviet Government and the central office of the Communist Party (the old POSDR) move to Moscow.
- In April Stalin is designated plenipotentiary to negotiate with the Rada of the Ukraine, since the Turks have taken Batum.

— On 17th July, the imperial family is executed at Ekaterinburg.

1920 — At the end of the year, the civil war finishes.

1922 — Lenin falls ill. In November, Lenin suffers a second attack, ending his political career. He is replaced by a triumvirate formed by Zinoviev, Kamenev and Stalin. Stalin will be the Secretary General of the Politburo.
— Lenin issues his political testament.

1923 — Stalin tells Trotsky, Zinoviev and Kamenev that Lenin has asked him for poison.
— Lenin asks for Trotsky's help against Stalin.
— On 9th March Lenin suffers a third and worse attack.

1924 — Lenin dies on 21st January.
— On 26th January Petrograd is given the name of Leningrad.

1927 — In October, the plenary session of the Central Committee and the Central Control Commission takes place. Zinoviev and Trotsky are expelled from the Central Committee. In November, Trotsky and Zinoviev are expelled from the Communist Party; Kamenev is removed from the Central Committee.

1928 — Trotsky is exiled to Alma-Ata. In 1929 he will even be exiled outside the USSR.

1929 — During this year, Stalin begins to govern like a true dictator.

1932 — Nadejda, Stalin's wife, dies (is assassinated?).

1934 — Kirov, Stalin's friend and his viceroy in Leningrad, is assassinated by Nikolaiev.
— Nikolaiev's trial, known as the Trial of the Fourteen, takes place. They are all condemned to death.

1936 — Trial of the Sixteen (Zinoviev, Kamenev and others). All the accused are executed.

1937 — Trial of the Seventeen. Thirteen of the accused are condemned to death. The remaining four suffer punishments of from eight to ten years' exile.

1938 — Trial of the Twenty-One. Eighteen are executed, among them Bujarin, Rikov and Kretinsky. Three are sentenced to prison.

1939 — On 4th May, Molotov takes charge of the portfolio of Foreign Affairs.
— In August, he signs the Molotov-Ribbentrop pact
— A new constitution is enacted.

— The Second World War breaks out.
— The invasion of the countries of the North begins.

1940 — On 20th May Leon Trotsky dies at his home in Mexico, assassinated by Ramon Mercader.

1941 — Hitler breaks the pact with Stalin and starts the invasion of the Soviet Union by the German armies.

1943 — The Tehran Conference takes place, attended by Stalin, Roosevelt and Churchill.

1944 — On 6th June the allied troops land in Normandy.
— Churchill returns to meet Stalin at the Kremlin. He is accompanied by Anthony Eden.

1945 — Europe is divided up at Yalta, on 3rd February 1945.
— The Soviet Armies begin the offensive from the Baltic to the Danube.
— In May the armistice is signed in Reims and in this way the war in Europe ends.
— The Potsdam Conference takes place over 15 days.

1947 — Stalin breaks off his relations with Tito and excludes Yugoslavia from the Kominform.

1948 — The blockade of Berlin, which does not end until 1949, is caused by Stalin.

1952 — The 19th Congress of the Soviet Communist Party takes place in Moscow in the month of October, the first since the end of the War.
— Stalin suffers the first attacks of arteriosclerosis.

1953 — Stalin suffers a brain haemorrhage on 2nd March.
— On 6th March the Soviets learn of the death of Joseph Stalin.

INDEX

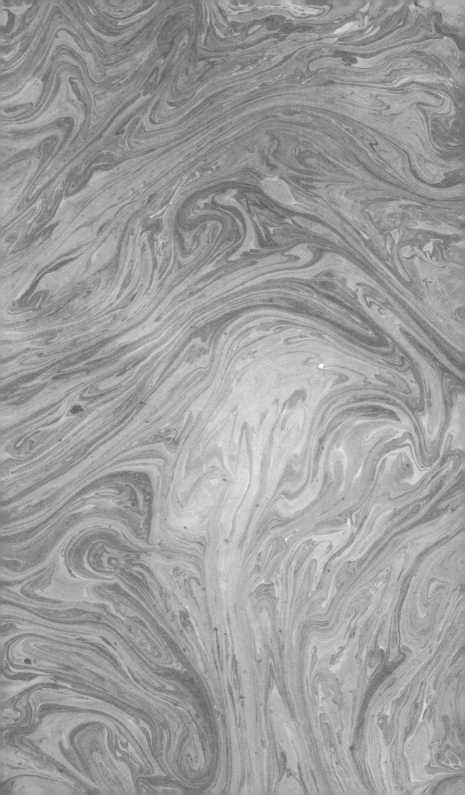